LET GO OF WHAT
YOU KNOW

LET GO OF WHAT YOU KNOW

AMELIA HENDREY

Wrate's Publishing

First published in 2023 by Wrate's Publishing

ISBN 978-1-7396165-9-5

Copyright © 2023 by Amelia Hendrey

Edited and typeset by Wrate's Editing Services

www.wrateseditingservices.co.uk

A CIP catalogue record for this book is available from the British Library.

For Dave, Piper and Angel, who have supported me through everything. Your love has made my books possible.

CONTENTS

INTRODUCTION

I would like to apologise in advance for this book, as it won't be as harrowing or as heart-wrenching as my first, *What Nobody Knew*. Although it's a follow-up, it's more light-hearted and funnier. Mainly, it's about who I have become as a person after the awful things I went through, the journey of writing the first book, how it was received and, finally, how I'm fitting into society and doing these days. It includes the diaries I kept while living through the Covid-19 pandemic.

You keep your guard up when so many bad things have happened to you, because you know that the bad stuff is not that far away, and that it could rear its ugly head at any given moment. You feel like you deserve the bad stuff because that's all you've ever known; you are tainted, and you are destined to have this horrible, black cloud looming overhead. But what if the bad stuff doesn't come? What if the black cloud moves on? Perhaps not forever, but just for a while. When that happens, it's hard to know how to react because the bad stuff is all you have ever known. You feel like you are damaged goods and are going to be classed as a victim forever. It's almost as if you have an imaginary label that the world can see, which you can never take off. The feeling of being emotionally tarnished never really goes away. You still have the memories, but you have learnt to put them in lots of little boxes in your head. These are tightly sealed with padlocks, and you hope that nothing triggers them to be unlocked. Unfortunately, one will burst open on occasion, and your head will be flooded with the relevant awful vision. The memory is loud and vivid, so you sing to yourself to try and block it out while you wrestle to get it back in the box.

You are determined to be normal and not to let the monsters define you. You utter the words to yourself: *I am not a victim. I am a survivor.*

You start living your life the way you should have done from the start, and you start learning how things should be rather than how they were. You're seeing the world through different eyes. Yes, the world is still scary, and it's still a challenge, but this time you have someone by your side to help you.

This is the story of my life now.

PART ONE

CHAPTER I

CATS

M oving in with Dave was a massive risk. I was young, and I didn't know the world as well as I should have done, but I liked him; he had kind eyes and a way about him that made me feel safe. And, despite all my flaws, he wanted to be with me.

At first, it was hard to adapt to my new surroundings. I was like a new pet brought home for the first time. I may not have gone as far as prowling round and smelling everything, but I was wary of the unknown.

After a while, I started to feel more at home. Dave had a cat. She was pure black, from her head to her toes, and very friendly. She adored Dave, and would sit high up on his chest, her face millimetres from his, purring loudly and rocking in time with her sounds of contentment. Her name was Isis. Dave said he named her this because he was visiting the Temple of Isis in Egypt when she was born. Dave had had her since she was a kitten, and she was 11 when I moved in. I love cats. Well, I love all animals. I would even go so far as to say I prefer them to people, but then I have met a few awful people in my time.

I was still close with my old friend Angel, and she came over to ours a lot. The three of us would go to clubs and restaurants in London. It was like we were the Three Musketeers. Angel wasn't sure about Dave at first – I think it was because she wanted to protect me – but after a while she let her guard down and realised he was one of the good guys.

A year into our relationship, I asked Dave if we could get a kitten. He wasn't sure Isis would cope with this: she was older and set in her ways, but we went looking in the hope that she would be fine with a new addition to the family. We drove to London to see a black and white kitten. She was sitting on the back of the sofa and was initially timid when I went to stroke her. The man selling her said she was the last of the litter, so we decided to go ahead and buy her. She mewed non-stop all the way home, and because of this we named her Shush. We bought her a lovely collar, a little scratching post, a litter tray and some kitten food. Then we introduced her to Isis, who was not impressed and constantly hissed her disgust. Shush wanted only to play with her. She would have these mad five minutes in which she would race up to Isis, stand high on her toes, run sideways and then throw herself onto the floor before darting away. Isis would get cross, hiss and bat her paws at Shush before giving up and finding somewhere high to sit, away from the scatty madness.

We decided to buy another kitten, so Shush would have a playmate. We visited a lady who had quite a few for sale, which she kept in an outdoor pen. I was sad when she told me the one I'd picked was already taken, but when I turned round, I saw Dave holding this tiny calico kitten. My heart melted and we took her home, only to realise she was a lot smaller than Shush and was probably the runt of the litter. She and Shush got on really well and became instant playmates. That night, they lay on our bed with us. Dave decided to call the new kitten Shakira, as he was a big fan of the singer. So that was our feline family: Isis, Shush and Shakira – all the girls together.

The next morning, we woke up to the smell of poo and realised Shakira had done her business on our bed. Her eyes were stuck together with gunk, and we suspected conjunctivitis. The poor mite was walking up and down our bed mewing because she couldn't see. Dave used a warm, wet cotton ball to clean the goo away from her eyes and she showed her gratitude by purring so loud I thought she was going to take off.

Life was good. Shush and Shakira constantly played together, racing from one end of the room to the other. They would occasionally get in Isis's way, but she would hiss, and then they'd carry on. When we let them out in the garden, Shakira ran up a tree and got stuck halfway up. Shush came to her rescue, using his mouth to carry her down by the scruff of her neck.

Soon it was time for the kittens to go on their first trip to the vets. Shakira was checked over first, and the vet confirmed our suspicion that she was indeed the runt of the litter. However, she was given a clean bill of health and was able to have her jabs. Now onto Shush. The vet commented on our happy, healthy little *boy*. Confused, I immediately pointed out that she was a girl. The vet looked at Shush again and said, "Nope, he's definitely a boy." I looked at Dave, who just shrugged his shoulders. So, Shush the girl was now Shush the boy. We could have given him a boy's name, but we thought Shush suited him, so we kept it.

A few months later, Shush's purr sounded funny, so we took him back to the vet's, where we were informed he had a polyp in the back of his throat, which was basically a growth that needed to be cut out. They didn't see many of these at the vet's, so they asked us if they could video the operation to show trainees, which we agreed to. We were so worried when he went in, but he came out like nothing had happened. Shakira missed him and showed how much by jumping on him and playing with him as soon as he got back to the house.

Nearly a year later, we booked the cats in to be spayed and neutered. Shush was first to have her procedure, but when it came to Shakira's turn we couldn't find her anywhere. She was still missing when Shush came home wearing his cone of shame. Beside ourselves with worry, we went out in search of her. We called out her name and rattled treats, but still nothing. A week later, we were in bed when she walked into our bedroom bedraggled, dirty and squeaking. We turned on the light, jumped out of bed and couldn't stop stroking and cuddling her. We immediately fed her and were just so happy she had come home. The next day, we phoned the vet to say she had returned, and we were informed there was a chance she could be pregnant due to the length of her absence. Lo and behold, she was. We created a 'birthing box' by cutting the front out of a cardboard box and placing a blanket inside it. Shakira showed no interest in it until she was about to give birth, when she promptly marched up to it and got inside. On 1st April, she gave birth to Ginge, Shrek and Zeus – all ginger and white. Of course, everyone I phoned with the good news thought it was an April fool's joke and didn't believe me.

As the years went on, we got more cats: Ooshee, Squishy, Sushi and Koshka. So, now we had a total of 10. I called them my Itty-bitty Kitty Committee. Due to my own upbringing, I had never seen myself having children – I didn't think I'd be capable of bringing up a child. Instead, I had a fur family, and I was happy to be their mum.

Did I plan to have 10 cats? No!

Would I have them all over again? Absolutely, in a heartbeat.

The experience has taught me that just like people, no cat is the same. Their personalities are different, and their perception of people and who they choose to be loyal to differs, too.

We suffered a few casualties along the way. Shakira broke her leg, so she had to have metal pins put in. She also had a heart murmur, and later she had to have all her teeth removed, but she never stopped loving me. From day one, she would sit on my lap at the same time every night like clockwork. She never missed a day.

Shush would wander into other people's houses and hang out with them for a while. People thought he was a stray and would feed him and take him in, but after a week he always came home again.

When we moved home, Shush, Shrek and Ginge were stolen and dumped in three different towns. We know they'd been "catnapped", shall we say, because they couldn't have walked to these separate locations by themselves and at the same time.

They were missing for three long months, and I was thinking the worst and going out of my mind. Then one day, our vet phoned us and said someone had found a cat. They scanned his microchip, and it was Shush. Fortunately, he was fine and came home safe and sound. The next to return was Shrek. He had wandered into some woman's house, and she had looked after him for two months. She even named him. Eventually, she took him to the vet to find out if he had an owner, as she thought they might be worried about him after such a long time. She had bought him toys and loved him very much, and she cried when we took him home. I felt really guilty, and a small part of me wanted to let her keep him, but Dave said he was our cat and he deserved to be in his rightful home with his brothers and his mum.

Lastly, someone found Ginge having a seizure under a car. They took him to a vet, where he was weighed and found to be seriously underweight. He'd been living on the streets, with no access to food or regular water, so his body had gone into survival mode and eaten into his body fat. As a result, he'd gone blind. The vet promised that if we gave them the say-so, they would do everything they could to save Ginge, but it was going to be a while before he got better, if he ever did. On top of his blindness, he also had some neurological problems, and Dave and I were faced with the dilemma of whether to try and save him or have him put to sleep. Dave said it wasn't fair to keep him alive because he was blind and had brain problems, and we wouldn't be able to give him a proper quality of life, but something in me didn't agree. When I first saw him at the animal hospital with all the tubes and drips in him, I stroked him through the bars of the cage, and he purred and did everything he could to rub against my hand. I just knew we had to do everything in our power to save him.

Ginge spent months at the animal hospital, and we made trips almost every week to see him. His sight came back, and he slowly started putting on weight. He had to learn to walk again, and he constantly fell over, but you could see he was getting stronger and had determination. He would still purr when he saw us and do everything he could to get up and come over. Once he was able to stand and walk without falling over, he was allowed to come home. He still walked with his head to one side, but the vet said that would maybe correct itself over time.

Six years on, and Ginge was still fighting fit. From time to time, his head would still flop to one side, but he remained as loving as ever. He passed away in 2020 at the grand old age of 17.

Isis reached a mature 18, and we think she might have suffered a stroke. She died in my arms on the way to the animal hospital. We put her in a little box with a flower and some cheese; she adored cheese.

Shush died in 2016. He was 15 and had developed a blood clot in the bottom of his back. He died while the vets were trying to save him. He had already passed by the time I got to him. He was wrapped in a towel, which I gently parted so I could see and stroke a tiny part of his fur as I said my goodbyes.

In that year, we also lost Shakira after she developed a lump on her neck. The vet said it was a tumour, but they couldn't cut it out because of its position. They said it would get bigger and she would very quickly get sick, which is precisely what happened. It broke my heart because every day I saw her getting a little bit slower and noticed how she was eating less. I knew it was time on the day she stopped eating and failed to get out of bed. I took her to the vet's, and they agreed that nothing else could be done for her. I snuggled up close to her as I cried my heart out and told her how much I loved her and how I'd always loved her. My heart was breaking into a million pieces, but I desperately wanted her to know what a good cat she was and that I loved her dearly. She lay there and purred while I sobbed on her, not wanting her to go. I was like a child who knew she was losing her friend for good, and every part of my body needed her to stay with me. I left the room, and the vet did what she had to do.

In 2018, we lost Shrek. Zeus left us in 2020, Squishy in 2021, and Ooshee in 2022. They all lived long, happy lives, and for that Dave and I are extremely grateful. I only wish I could have that time back. We are classed as a normal cat household now, as we only have three remaining feline friends. It's not the same and there is a quietness where they all once were.

My heart is still broken, but I have found a way to keep moving forward. In February 2019, I decided to set up my own cat sitting business. In 17 years, I have owned 11 cats, so I think it's safe to say I know a lot about them. I have seen them experience all sorts of different injuries and ailments, I know the signs to look out for if they are unwell, I have administered medication and I am an all-round cat person – a cat geek, if you wish. So, I thought I would use my knowledge for good and start my own feline enterprise.

My business would include going to people's houses and visiting their cats while they were away on holiday, making sure they were OK, feeding and watering them, changing their litter trays and cuddling them, plus any other tasks the client asked me to do. I started off by coming up with a name for my new company. I picked *The Cat Sitter* because it seemed simple and to the point. Next, I sent away for a DBS check. This piece of paper proves that I have no criminal convictions, and it's something I can show to the client to give them peace of mind about who they are hiring. I also purchased public liability insurance in the event of an accident in their home while they were away. Next, I got some business cards and posters printed up and created a Facebook page. I decided on a uniform, and I even had an advertisement emblazoned across my car. I was all set. Over the next couple of months, I picked up quite a few clients. I was on my way and doing a job I loved. What more could I want?

Almost four years on (at the time of writing), and business is booming. I have regular clients and look after numerous cats. They all have their own characters and likes and dislikes. I've been promoting *What Nobody Knew* alongside working on two more books. That's why this book – book two – has taken so long to be published. I've been juggling lots of different things and loving every minute of it. Of course, I've also been running a house while being a parent and a wife. Who knew I could juggle so many things? Having created two businesses from scratch, I have a lot to feel proud about.

CHAPTER 2
WORK

When I moved in with Dave, my benefits stopped, and he suggested that maybe I should get a job. I'd never had a job before, but I was determined to live the way everyone else did.

I started off in retail, on the shop floor. I had no idea people could get so angry over minor things, screaming for the manager when you can't help them and blaming your incompetence for whatever is not right. Luckily, that was only temporary Christmas work until I found something else.

Next, I tried working in a pub. Serving drinks and food couldn't be that hard, could it? Well, drunk people making vile comments while half-cut did not sit well with me, so I moved swiftly on.

So, what can I say about telesales? It's all about trying to sell people stuff they really don't want, while being questioned over how you got their number. There were only so many times I could take people telling me to f**k off before concluding this was not for me and that it was time to move on. Again.

There were loads of things I wanted to do that I didn't have the qualifications or opportunity to go for: film critic, TV extra, a reviewer of things, veterinary nurse, helping in a cattery. These were my dreams, but for now, I needed to be realistic. The one thing I was sure about was that I'd had enough of working with the general public, so I decided to try something else

I applied for a warehouse job and was offered the position following an initial interview. I was extremely nervous. I had never worked in a warehouse before, but I was trained up and the people were friendly. The bonus was that I didn't have to deal with customers, just customer orders. I was good at my job, and I really enjoyed it, too. So, now I had a job, what next?

Dave said he would help me pay for driving lessons so I could get myself to work and back and gain some independence. These lessons were really daunting at first, but I stayed focused and passed my driving test first time. I have been a motorist for over a decade now, and the two main things I have learnt are: don't watch two pigeons fighting in your rear-view mirror, no matter how much they are going at it, because you will nearly crash into a tree; and while on the subject of trees, if one is hanging over the road, don't try and drive through it because the branches you assumed were twigs will take your wing mirror clean off. In general, avoid trees.

I loved being with Dave. He made me feel warm and fuzzy inside and, most importantly, he made me feel safe. He had a calmness about him. He never shouted or panicked about stuff, and it always seemed that in general, he just had his life together. He had started his business from scratch all by himself, and he seemed to know about the world. He didn't have a lot of friends, and he was happy that way. He loved travelling the world, and he had been to many countries. After a while, I was no longer a *me* and an *I*, but an *us* and a *we*. *We* had dinner, *we* went shopping, *we* watched TV, and *we* met up with our friends. It felt so easy and simple. As a result, I became a much stronger person. I was no longer a victim; I was an *us*.

I was no stranger to rejection, pain and suffering, but this new path was different, like a breath of fresh air. I still had lots to learn, but I would wake up feeling loved, cared for and completely happy.

I had lots of friends at the warehouse, and the only downside was that I worked the night shift. Working nights is hard, and I couldn't move over to the day shift until a vacancy became available. So, I would wake up at 4 pm in the afternoon to start work at 6.45 pm. I wouldn't leave again until 5.45 am, sometimes later if there was overtime.

When I woke up for breakfast, Dave was having his dinner. When I came home to go to bed, he was getting up for work. It was like I was living my life back to front, and I felt very lonely. I couldn't phone Dave on my lunch break because he would already be in bed asleep. During winter, I would go to work in the dark and come home in the dark, so the only time I saw daylight was either just before I left for work or on my days off. Summer was not good for daytime sleeping, as the sun would be shining, and people would be out mowing their lawns and making a racket. I hated working the night shift, and I only hope I'll never have to do it again.

After a couple of years, I moved over to the day shift. On my first morning, I felt like I was in a brand-new job and had a brand-new way of thinking. Things didn't feel so backward anymore. I continued to enjoy and be good at my job. Who knew this would be the start of some amazing things to come?

I'd been in my job for many years when, one morning, I

woke up and realised I felt different. I went to leave the house and just couldn't do it. For no apparent reason, anxiety had struck, and I couldn't shift it. I'd been fine the previous day, but now I felt a wave of uncontrollable fear. I couldn't breathe and my heart was beating so hard it felt as if it was going to leave my body. A hard pressure of air surrounded my head, which pulsated with a 'whoomph whoomph' noise. My palms were sweaty, and I felt as if I was going to be sick. This feeling lasted 15 minutes or more, before all my symptoms disappeared as quickly as they had arrived.

There were similar episodes, and the worst thing was, I couldn't predict when they were going to happen. They seemed to come out of nowhere. I only found out later, after seeing a doctor, that feeling uncomfortable or a little bit anxious would trigger these panic attacks. Whenever I felt one coming on, I would go outside and breathe in giant gulps of air. My skin would feel like it was burning, and the cold air provided some relief. Once outside, everything slowed down to the point where normality returned, and it was as if I'd just stepped off a rollercoaster. I started to avoid planning stuff, because I worried I'd have a panic attack and have to shoot outside or go home. If I did do something, nine times out of 10, I would have a panic attack because I was nervous about having a panic attack. It was a vicious cycle.

People who have never experienced a panic attack can't understand what they're like, and why should they? Before I started having them, I wouldn't have known how to help someone going through one. Occasionally, people would say things like, "Take deep breaths, in through your nose and slowly out through your mouth." Or they'd fetch me a glass of water to drink. I know they were only trying to be helpful, but none of this changed anything. The panic attacks passed when they were ready to, some quicker than others.

Eventually, I went to the doctor and asked for something to make them stop. First, I had to have blood tests to find out what was causing them. Blood tests terrify me. For some reason, they make me feel woozy and scared. So, having the tests to find out the cause of my panic attacks set off a panic attack. Not fun. Luckily, nothing showed up, so the doctor gave me some medication to help. It worked a treat.

To date, it has been 10 years since my last panic attack.

* * *

You can eat well and live well, but that doesn't make you immune to the inevitable. If death doesn't catch you, it will catch your neighbour, your friend, your loved one – just to remind you that time is precious and unpredictable. We all want to do well in life, and we hope we will be remembered for the right reasons, but time moves on, and after our loved ones have followed along behind us, we will become a distant memory. But being in possession of this knowledge doesn't prevent us from trying our hardest not to be forgotten while we are living, mainly because that's the only thing we can do.

No one I have loved has died. People have died, yes, but not any that I have really cared about. My dad was a monster, and you can't love someone when they constantly inflict pain on you. When he died, I felt relief rather than grief. When my mother died, I grieved for what I should have had rather than what she was, so I never experienced the rip-roaring loss of someone I truly love passing away.

This means I struggle to understand that feeling when it happens to someone else. I know what they are going through, but I can't relate to it.

When Dave lost his mother, I watched him break in front of me. She had colon cancer and quickly deteriorated. Dave adored his mother. He and his brothers grew up poor, but Dave always used to tell me that although they had nothing, they always had love.

His father left when he was very young, so his mother took on the role of two parents, while working two jobs. Later, she remarried, and her husband moved into the house. Dave didn't really care for this man, but he was happy that his mother was happy. Sadly, her husband passed away when she was in her sixties. She was in her eighties when the cancer diagnosis was confirmed, and because of her advancing age she decided against treatment, as she didn't want to string out the inevitable. Her age didn't show on her face, but her body was frail. Throughout her life, she'd always said that under no circumstances was she to go into a nursing home. Dave did everything he could to help her keep her wish, but the hospital where she was receiving her care didn't have the bed space to keep her indefinitely, so our choice was taken away from us. A date was set for her to move into a nursing home. The night before she was due to leave the hospital, she died in her sleep. She got her wish in the end.

I have never seen Dave so broken, and I hope I will never see him like that again. He was a shell of a person, and I could see the immense sorrow in his blue eyes. He struggled to believe that his mother was no longer with us, and I remember him saying to me, "I've never not a had a mother before." That phrase sums it up, because what *do* you do when you don't have a mother anymore? He used to call her every day to chat, and the void she left was huge. Throughout this devastating time, I comforted him the only way I knew how. I held him, talked to him about his mum and made time just to 'be' with him. Even now, Dave still misses his mum and talks about her often. I'm guessing time helps, as do the tiny distractions of life. You don't necessarily feel complete, and you don't forget, but your wounds heal just a tiny bit every day, and that is how you are able to carry on.

Am I scared of dying or losing a loved one? Of course I am! Who isn't? And the fact that it's out of my control makes it even scarier. No one wants to die, but none of us gets a choice. All I can do is to ensure the people in my life know that I love them, and that I always will.

CHAPTER 3
MARRIAGE

After nine years, Dave asked me to marry him. Wow, I was marriage material… who knew! We had a wonderful wedding, and all our friends joined us in celebrating. We ate fantastic food, drank and danced, and the room was a sea of smiles. In one day, I went from a Miss to a Mrs, and I loved that Dave was now my husband. I didn't realise there was so much to organise for a wedding. There are all these tiny details that are easy to forget about. We didn't have a massive do, but it was good enough for us. I wore a pretty dress and Dave looked dashing all suited and booted.

Then Dave decided that we should go on our honeymoon, as I had never been on holiday before. The thought of being in another country made me uneasy. What if something happened there and I couldn't get home? What if I lost Dave and couldn't find him again? What if the plane developed a problem and we crashed or got stranded somewhere? Eventually, I decided that worrying wasn't going to get me anywhere, so I pushed my concerns to the back of my mind. Dave is a culture vulture, and he likes to go on tours and look at what the different countries have to offer. I didn't fancy the thought of trudging around in the heat, so I asked if we could have a beach holiday and just lay on the sand next to the sea. Dave agreed on the condition that on our next holiday, we would do culture. Deal.

We chose Lanzarote, asked a neighbour to look after the Itty-Bitty Kitty Committee, packed our suitcases and headed to the airport. We had lots of waiting to do before we were finally able to board the plane. The take-off made my tummy flip, but it wasn't as bad as I had been expecting. When the plane landed, which I was very relieved about, the doors opened, and a wave of heat hit us. This was a shock, as it had been incredibly cold when we boarded the plane in London.

Our hotel was perfect. I was still nervous, but I told myself I had earned this time to relax. Besides, we were here now, so there was no turning back. Typically, I soon found a cat to stroke in the hotel grounds, which was an amazing start to our holiday, and then we headed to the beach. The sea breeze was heavenly; the air smelled cleaner somehow, enough to make you want to breathe it deep into your lungs. The beach was beautiful, the sun blazed in the sky, waves of warmth gently massaged my face, and the sea was clear blue. Palm trees gently swayed, and everyone looked happy. We walked down towards the sea and paid for sun loungers on which to park my butt. Dave lay beside me, and we were content in that moment and the amazing atmosphere. Later, I had a dip in the sea, and we drank cocktails. We stayed at the beach for most of the day, the light wind taking away the heat from the day. It was only when we got back to our hotel room that we realised how burnt we were. We had stayed on the beach for far too long, and now we hurt. We couldn't even have a shower, because the droplets of water on our skin felt like knives. To try and bring down the temperature of our skin, we wrapped ourselves in soaking wet towels, but we could feel the heat radiating through the material. After being laid up in our hotel room for two days, we hobbled off to a chemist and bought some cream and spray to put on our wounds. Now that we were 50 percent healed, it was time to carry on with our holiday, though we made sure we wore hats and covered up.

We found pamphlets in the hotel lobby advertising swimming with sea lions and camel rides. We both signed up for the camel ride, but as Dave wasn't a fan of sea lions, he said he'd sit that one out. The camel ride was amazing. I'd had no idea how big these desert animals are in real life – or how smelly! I loved them all the same. We went for a long ride on the sand and when it was time to dismount, I gave my one a hug. Yep, I hugged a camel. I thought the activity was a bit cruel because the camels take tourist for rides all day, just for our pleasure. I would have been quite happy to have stood and stroked it.

Next, I went for my swim with the sea lion. I had to wear a wetsuit with a huge inflatable jacket over it. The rules were not to touch the sea lion unless you were told to, and not to splash, as they really don't like being splashed. We all had to stand in a line in the pool and wait until the sea lion came out. As I'm short, my feet didn't touch the bottom. So, when the sea lion finally emerged from its enclosure out the back, I started to float away! Of course, I couldn't swim forward because that would mean splashing, which I'd been explicitly instructed not to do. Our sea lion guide asked me if I was OK and I replied, "Yes, it's just my feet don't touch the floor." He asked the others to grab my inflatable jacket and pull me back in, and he then got us all to link arms and hold onto me, to stop me from floating away again. How to make friends and influence people.

The sea lion came close to us and gave us all a kiss. Then the instructor got us to lay on our backs while the sea lion pushed us around the pool by our feet. We were even able to have a cuddle with him. As I wrapped my arms around him, I could feel his sheer strength; he also felt very rubbery. I don't know what I'd been expecting, but I guess I thought sea lions would be smaller, and here this one was bigger than me! The sea lion proceeded to jump over us, swim around us, and splash us. Yes, the sea lion was allowed to splash us, but we couldn't splash him! It was an amazing experience, and I'd do it all over again in a heartbeat. I loved every moment.

For the remainder of our stay in Lanzarote, we watched shows, ate fantastic food, saw the sights, went swimming and relaxed. I found more cats, as you do. I was in my element. I couldn't have asked for a better first holiday.

CHAPTER 4

OUR DAUGHTER

I never wanted children. I wasn't very maternal, and a big part of my thought process around the subject was to do with my belief that I was bad inside. Because my parents did things to me, I thought their depravity was somehow genetic and that I was destined to be bad, too. I couldn't have lived with myself if that was the case. I didn't want to do to a child what my parents had done to me, so the easiest solution was not to have one in the first place.

By this point, I'd been with my husband Dave for 12 years and we shared everything. I always spoke to him about how I felt about life, and one day we were having a conversation and it came up that if, God forbid, anything happened to him, I would be alone. My friends would all have families of their own, and although I would still have their friendship, I wouldn't have anyone to call my own. I thought about this, and it shook me a little bit. No one wants to be alone, with no family and only friends. Is that what I really wanted?

So, I said to Dave that maybe we should think about having a child. That way, if anything happened to him, I wouldn't be alone, and I would sort of have a purpose in life. I know it's a selfish way of thinking, but that's what we discussed. We thought about it for a few months, and we even wrote a list of pros and cons. How much would having a child cost? What would we need? Would the cats be OK with a tiny new family member around? What changes would we need to make to our lifestyle? We agreed to change some things, and we hoped we could be the parents we wanted to be. I was scared because I didn't want to make a mistake. I didn't know if I could love a child, as I had never loved one before. Also, what if the child didn't love me? What would I do then? The main fear in the back of my mind was that I had no solid parental figure to guide me, so any mistakes would be on me. I never knew my mother, so I didn't know if I had any of her traits or mannerisms. I lost her twice in my lifetime, and I didn't even have her to start with. I never knew what sort of personality she had or whether I was like her in any way, so there was always that missing piece of me. I knew who my father was, and when any similarities with him showed up I would squash them down and make them disappear. I didn't want to be like him at all. I hated myself for being like him.

After much thought, I explained my anxieties to Dave, and he helped to ease them. He said that I had him, so we would make any mistakes together, though if I thought deep in my heart that I was going to be anything like my parents, then we shouldn't have a child. I thought about it long and hard, and I was determined I was going to be nothing like them.

Next thing I knew, 'we' were pregnant. I did a test at 4 am before heading off to work. The complete shock of seeing it was positive brought the reality home. The happiness came later, but right then I was in a daze and unsure what to do. I experienced a multitude of emotions all at once: happiness, excitement and fear. It was overwhelming. When I spoke to the doctor, she said that I had to come off my anxiety medication because I couldn't take it while carrying a child. I did this straight away, and I haven't had a panic attack since.

Being pregnant was a nice experience, but it was also nerve-racking. There are lots of things you can't eat, and some things you can't drink. You must be healthy to ensure the baby is healthy. You slowly get bigger, and then it feels like you're losing your identity. People comment on your belly before asking how you are. There are only so many times a day you can hear people say, "You've gotten big" and "Not long now!" I know people have the best intentions and they are only showing an interest, but if they realised how many people have already said it that day, then maybe they would choose to say something else!

We never went to antenatal classes; we thought we would just read stuff online instead. We made the spare bedroom into a nursery and kitted it out with everything the baby would need. We were good to go. For a tiny human being that doesn't do much other than eat and sleep, there is a whole bunch of stuff to buy.

I turned 30 while pregnant. Angel and I had always spoken about this milestone, back when it seemed such a long way away, and all the things we would do before reaching this magic number. Well, 30 was now here and I was expecting.

A few friends called, including Angel, to ask what I was doing for my birthday and if I fancied going out for dinner. I didn't want to go, I just wanted to sit on my fat pregnant butt at home away from everyone. Going out seemed too much of an effort, so I explained that we would celebrate my birthday the following year when I'd no doubt be feeling livelier. Dave was at work, so I was home alone and I was happy with that. I had a shower and lay on my bed watching my stomach move as my 'Karate Kid' child had a kick-about. I loved watching it go kick-crazy, as it was one way of knowing my baby was OK. That day my baby was kicking me a happy birthday, and that was all I needed.

Later, I went downstairs, lay on the sofa and turned on the TV. After an hour, the doorbell rang, and when I opened it, I found Angel standing there holding balloons and a cake. "You're finally 30," she said to me. "So, you are *not* spending your birthday on your own."

This act of spontaneity is why I'm so proud to call Angel my friend.

The two of us watched a film and ate the cake. Between mouthfuls, we chatted about our adolescence and how we'd thought the big 3-0 would be life-changing, and how it really wasn't. In fact, it wasn't what we had expected at all. We spoke about how maybe 50 would feel different because then we would be nearer 60, and how by 60, we would be a lot wiser and more knowing. (We shall see, but I doubt it!) Right then, I was just happy I'd made it to 30.

A month later, Dave came with me for the 12-week scan. It went well, and we got to see the baby and hear the heartbeat. Who would have thought a grainy black and white image could make you so proud? On one of the later images, you could see the baby looking at the camera and kicking out at it. That scan picture was a keeper.

I carried on going to work throughout my pregnancy, which is where one of the strangest things to ever happen to me occurred. We sat behind computers along a counter, and the warehouse workers would come in and we would hand them gloves, boots and high-vis jackets – basically, everything they would need for their shift. One day, a female worker came in and handed me some keys she had found, which I put on a desk behind me. A few hours later, a man came up to the counter. Without even looking up from my computer screen, I grabbed the keys and handed them to him. "These are yours," I said.

He looked really dumbfounded and replied, "You're right, but I didn't even know I had lost them. How did you know they are mine?"

"Because they smell like you," I said.

He looked really confused, so I explained how when the lady had handed me the keys, I noticed they had an oily, musty smell. This matched the man's own aroma, which I noticed as soon as he came towards my desk. Without my even thinking about it, my brain had put two and two together. I think the man thought I was a little strange, as he couldn't detect the smell I was talking about, but he was grateful to get his keys back and I think I provided him with some entertainment that day.

This happened to me a lot when I was pregnant, and I haven't been able to do it since.

Pregnancy does strange things to you.

By the end of my pregnancy, I had learned that I can survive on just two hours' sleep a night and put a person I haven't even met yet first. I realised that as my child grew up, I wouldn't be able to answer all her questions about life, because I don't know all the answers. I also knew that I couldn't promise her that people wouldn't lie to her or hurt her. The only promise I knew I could make and keep was to love her unconditionally.

Everybody experiences childbirth differently. Some labours are extreme, and some are what you might like to call manageable. Either way, everyone has a story to tell because having a baby is an amazing journey.

As I mentioned earlier, I hadn't been to any antenatal classes, as I thought that I could just breeze my way through it. All I knew was that it was going to hurt and that it was going to hurt a lot. Was I scared? Completely. Was I ready? Not a chance.

I came downstairs one morning after experiencing terrible back pain. I tried to take my mind off it by watching some TV, but the pain just kept getting worse, and it was now shooting round to the front of my stomach. *What is this baby doing?* I thought. I tried lying in different positions on the sofa, but I just couldn't get comfy. Then I started to cry because it had dawned on me that I was in labour. The baby was on its way.

Dave came straight home from work and took me to the hospital, where they gave me pain relief. This made the agony stop completely, and I was able to recover myself emotionally. But when the drugs wore off, the pain was so much worse. Eight hours of pain and getting into multiple positions followed. At one point, I thought I had delivered the baby, but my midwife informed me that no, it was just my waters breaking. I went to the toilet, and when I got up, I saw blood in the pan. I screamed that there was something wrong with my child, but the midwife informed me that no, this was just 'my show', a blob of mucus that comes away from the cervix just before labour starts. I really should have read up on everything and gone to those antenatal classes. Lesson learned.

When the contractions arrived, they really weren't pleasant. Sharp, hard and fast are the only words I can think of to describe it. Every time I had one, I would squeeze my legs together and bend at my knees. I don't know why I did this, I guess it was a coping mechanism. I remember the nurse telling me that I needed to stop doing it as I was blocking the baby's exit.

To make matters worse, I projectile vomited over the midwife – more than once. (If you're reading this, again I am truly sorry.) I didn't even feel the sickness coming; it was like something from a comedy sketch, and I threw up on her from head to toe. An hour after she had changed her uniform, I did it again. At that moment, I felt the pain of labour and the pain of humiliation. That poor, poor woman.

Dave held my hand throughout. I had no control over what was happening inside my body, and that terrified me. I had no choice but to go with it. Eventually, the baby came down and it felt like everything in my body was breaking. When her head came out, it felt like I was on fire. My insides tore as her body followed, and she turned so her shoulders were facing upright. I just remember screaming. The rest of her just sort of fell out after that. My whole body jolted from the shock, and I couldn't stop it. I felt the tug on the umbilical cord as they laid her on my chest, but I couldn't enjoy it because of the jolting. She started crying and I knew it was finally over, and that I must find some strength from somewhere to appreciate the moment.

Childbirth feels like you are having every bone in your body broken all at the same time. It's not exactly an experience I would recommend, but there is no feeling like the moment you hold your baby in your arms. It is the most amazing, heart-warming, bubbly feeling, and all the horrors of labour just melt away.

They cut the umbilical cord and gave her to Dave. She was so small and fragile, and she was ours. I couldn't stop looking at her lovely little face and her wrinkly feet; she was perfect. They wrapped her up in a soft, canary yellow blanket, and she was quite content. Meanwhile, I – not so content – was wheeled off to get stitched up.

Afterwards, I was wheeled back to Dave and our teeny-tiny new baby. She was happy to be carried around by her proud daddy. A nurse put her on me to feed and afterwards placed her in a little cot next to my bed. She told me to get some sleep, as I needed to rest. Dave went home to freshen up and said he would come back to see us later. I tried to sleep, but the moment I closed my eyes they bolted straight open again. I was terrified the baby might need something and that I wouldn't know what to do. So, I lay there with my hand in her cot. I touched her tiny fingers and just watched her. Then suddenly, I realised I needed to pee. I tried to get up, but this was hard because I was so sore. Eventually, I managed to haul myself up and race to the toilet. But by the time I got there, it was too late, and there was already a trail of pee behind me. I got some tissue and tried to bend down to clear it up, but attempting to get that low was agony. I tried different ways of doing it, but I just couldn't reach the floor. Then the baby started to cry. I went over and said, "It's OK, hi, hello." But she continued wailing. I wanted more than anything to pick her up, but she was so small. I stroked her face, but she cried even more. Panicking, I pulled the cord for the midwife. When she came in, I burst into tears. "I'm sorry, I don't know what happened but I peed on the floor," I sobbed. "And I want to hold the baby, but I'm not sure how."

The midwife (the same one I vomited on) was amazing. She cleaned up the pee and told me not to worry about it. Then she helped me to get the baby dressed and to feed her. Semi-normality was restored. It's people like my midwife who make the world a better place. She made a scary situation manageable. The baby stopped crying and went back to sleep. I remained absolutely petrified. I felt like she was made of glass and that one false move would cause her to smash.

The love I felt for her was so intense; I had never felt love like it before. It felt like my heart had swelled and doubled in size. She had a little button nose and lots of dark hair, and the top of her ear was folded over and stuck from where she had been lying on it inside me. I had never experienced such an overwhelming swell of love for another person.

Dave came back a few hours later, and I was so relieved to see him. Now we could be scared together. We put this fragile little person in a car seat and drove off, ready to start our lives as a trio.

I stared at her all the way home. I had waited nine long months for her to be in our life, and here she finally was. As we pulled into our street, I imagined it to be littered with people celebrating our achievement. Because to me, this was the biggest achievement of my entire life. I thought of them waving at our car, desperate to meet the new person we had created. But no, there was no street party, and no one was waiting outside our house. Everyone was just carrying on with their day-to-day routine.

After having my baby, I was pretty much housebound. I hurt a lot and could only walk slowly. Days and nights merged into one, and I was more tired than I had ever been. I was too emotionally unstable to face the world and only had strength for the baby. I was overwhelmed, underwhelmed, emotional and scared all at the same time.

The first night was really tough. We had got through the day feeding and changing her, and we finally put her down to sleep. But throughout the night, she kept throwing up mucus; we were so close to calling an ambulance, but she wasn't crying and seemed content. Finally, we decided to call the midwife unit, and they said it was normal and nothing to worry about. Even so, we both stayed awake all night. We were terrified until daybreak, when the arrival of the first light made things feel less daunting.

We muddled through the baby stage until we had a routine in place. We put her on formula milk, and we said under no circumstances would we give her a dummy, but through being exhausted and after a full night of crying, we finally broke and gave her one, which she was happy about.

I was in an alien situation. I knew I had to protect and love my daughter, but I was frightened of all the everyday dangers that might harm her simply because she was so tiny. Everything was a little scary: the first nappy change, the mucus, the constant worry, the feeds and the overwhelming feeling of, *Wow, I just created a tiny human being that is incapable of doing anything for herself. Within reason, everything she comes into contact with is dangerous, and it's my job as her mother to keep her alive.*

We learnt as we went, and apart from being unimaginably tired, we were still up for the challenge, even when our baby went for her heel-prick test and the midwife looked at me and asked why her nappy was on the wrong way round. I just smiled and shrugged. In my defence, I would like to say you have two options with nappies – animals on the front or animals on the back. It would have helped if inside the nappy was some writing that said, "This goes at the back", or something along those lines. There wasn't, so I guessed. The fact that it had been pointed out meant I had guessed wrong. The tabs of the nappy go on the back not the front. Thank you, midwife, for your input on that one.

I was a scared, fragile new mum. If you made a mistake, your baby could die. And if parenting wasn't daunting enough, there are so many rules. Put them to sleep on their backs; don't let them sleep for too long or they could dehydrate; always make your feeds up fresh because of bacteria. You're a scared mum, and the rules blow your mind. So, I started writing stuff down, just so I wouldn't forget. Because when the baby cried, I would lose my train of thought. The midwives said sleep when the baby sleeps, so you can rest and get your energy back. But I didn't follow their advice because I was too scared. What if she needed me and I didn't wake up to help her? That fear alone kept me awake.

My favourite phrase when the baby was small was, "Is it normal?" Because nothing ever seemed normal, and everything that seemed abnormal was amplified because I was so tired. So, Google became my best friend. This was the place to go whenever I felt unsure about something. It would help put my mind at rest, and it gave me a little bit of security in an unknown world. I also didn't feel like I was bothering people with my mountain of questions.

When the baby was born, Angel wrote her a lovely card.

Dear 'The Princess',

The day you were born was so special and exciting; we had waited for your arrival for nine months. Your mummy sent me a photo of you as soon as you arrived, and I couldn't believe how beautiful you were. You are the most gorgeous newborn I have ever seen. I hope you will allow me to be your auntie (a crazy auntie). You must be thinking why crazy? Well, you will find out.

I love you so much already. xxxx

The first time Dave left me alone with the baby was when she was 10 days old. He said he would only be a couple of hours, and although I was a bit nervous, I had a feed/sleep routine sorted, so what was the worst that could happen? Everything started off well. I sang her nursery rhymes and played hand puppets and then it was milk time, so she had her feed, and I took her upstairs for a new nappy and a change of clothes. I put her on the changing table and took off her onesie and undid her nappy. At this point, she started to poo, so I put the nappy back in place to give her some privacy. But this poo went on for what seemed like forever, and it came out like toothpaste being squeezed from the tube. Then suddenly, she started being sick because I had laid her down too soon after her milk. She needed to be upright for half an hour or she would be milk sick, and I had clearly forgotten this. I went to pick her up but then remembered I couldn't because of what was coming out at the other end. So, I got a tissue to wipe her mouth with, and in doing so, I accidentally knocked the umbilical cord peg off her belly button, which started to bleed a little bit. Feeling totally defeated, I started to cry and tell her what a terrible mum I was and how she'd drawn the short straw in getting me for her mum. I then got a grip, changed her bum, put tissue on her belly button, wrapped the peg up in a wipe, changed her clothes and picked her up for a hug. "That was a disaster, wasn't it?" I said. "I promise I will try harder."

A couple of weeks later, cabin fever set in, and I decided to take her for a walk. When we passed the park, I thought I'd take her in and show her around.

"I can't put you on the swings because you will fall straight through the slats," I explained to her. "I can't put you on the seesaw because we must be a similar body weight for it to work, so that's clearly not going to work. I can't put you on the slide because you're so small it might feel like Alton Towers to you, and you might bump your head. So, are you OK watching for now? Because I am if you are."

The more I cared for my baby, the less scary it became. But it remained hard work. Really hard work. Was it worth it? Definitely.

The list of learning curves was endless: teething, sleepless nights, how long till she feeds, how long she feeds for, and so on. And then there's learning that baby poop comes in lots of different colours, and that's not always something you need to freak out over.

And then there are the rules. No co-sleeping, no sleeping on her front, don't let her sit in a bouncer too long or it will ruin her spine... All these rules just made me panic more. I was also told to keep any small objects out of her way because they were a choking hazard. Then, when she was just over a year, we took her for a check-up and her hand-eye coordination was tested. They wanted her to put a bead on the end of a piece of string, and they asked if I had let her do this at home. I replied no, as clearly she could choke on the bead and the string, so why would I have them at home?

Throughout the whole time of parenting a baby and then a toddler, I learned to expect the unexpected. There was always something. When she was two and a half, I walked into the bathroom to find her drinking toilet water from a spoon. I freaked out and phoned NHS111. They advised me to keep an eye on her and to look out for vomiting and anything that was out of character. If any of these things did happen, then I was to take her straight to the hospital. I then phoned Dave at work, and he said, "Well, at least she has etiquette and wasn't using her hands." She was fine, by the way. All that worry for nothing.

My daughter loved her dummy; it was her favourite thing in the whole world. Whenever she lost it, which she did on a regular basis, the world would come to an end, and we would have to turn the house upside down looking for it. We kept her cot in our room until she was eight months old, and if her dummy fell out while she was sleeping, she would bang her feet up and down until someone put it back in her mouth. We used to call it the dummy dance. In the end, we had a total of seven dummies: two in her bed, two in the car, two downstairs and a backup one, which we kept in a special hiding place in case we lost all the others.

As the years went by, I would like to say it got easier, but it was different rather than easier. When you finally overcame one challenge, another one presented itself.

Because of the abuse I'd suffered, I have never left my daughter in anyone else's care. It's safe to say I have severe trust issues. But if that's what I must do to protect her, then so be it. After all, that's my job. I will never say to my child the dreadful things that were said to me when I was little. My girl will never be told, "Keep crying and I'll give you something to cry about," or "Stop talking or I'll smack the chatty out of you."

She will always be – and feel – loved.

* * *

I know this chapter is all about our daughter, but I have one more story about a cat. It does relate to her, though, and you'll find out why when you get to the end…

Back when I worked night shifts, I was driving home one morning when I saw the car in front of me hit a cat. I watched in horror as he tumbled through the air, hit the road and then landed on the grass verge. The driver just carried on. I slammed on my brakes, put my hazards on and rushed over to the poor animal's side. There was a wire fence between us, but I managed to crouch down to his level. There was blood in his mouth, and he was hissing at me. I understood that he was angry, and I didn't want to grab him in case he had internal injuries. Every time I tried to stroke his white fur, which was streaked with patches of grey, he would lash out at me and hiss, so I sat next to him and gently explained that it wasn't me that hit him, and that he needed to go to the animal hospital, because I didn't want him to die. If he just allowed me to put him in my car, everything would be OK. I must have sat there for 15 minutes trying to gain his trust. I continued talking to him, and he eventually let me stroke his head and stopped hitting out and hissing. Then he started panting, which I knew wasn't a good sign. Thinking quickly, I stood up, leaned over the fence and grabbed him by the scruff of the neck. I lifted him clean over the wire and then cradled him in my arms. Luckily, I happened to have a blanket in my boot, which I used to wrap him up, before laying him in the passenger footwell of my car. I then drove him to a nearby animal hospital. When I arrived, I explained to the vet what had happened and said it wasn't my cat and that I didn't know who it belonged to. I gave him a kiss on the head, and they took him away. I then filled out a form with my details, telling the vet that if he didn't have an owner, I would be happy to take him. I left praying he would be OK.

A week later, I received a phone call from a lady asking if I was the person who had saved her cat. I said I was, and she asked if it was me who had hit him. I explained that he had been struck by the vehicle in front of me. She said that the cat's name was Max and that he didn't live far from where he had been hit. The vet had fixed him, and he was almost fully recovered. She had decided to keep him inside from now on, and she was so grateful I'd saved him, as most people wouldn't have been so kind. She then asked for my address, as she wanted to send me a thank you card and show her appreciation. I said she didn't have to – I was just glad he was OK – but I gave her my address anyway and we said our goodbyes. A few days later, I received a lovely letter from the lady, which read:

Dear Amelia,
Just a small gift to say a big thank

you for rescuing my cat, Max. You are
a very kind lady, and I can't put into
words the things I really want to say
to you. Max is a rescue cat. I've had
him three years now and I really love
him. We also have a female cat called
Ellie, who is now 14 years old. She is
also a rescue. You are most welcome to
come and see Max if you ever feel like
it. Thank you once again for your help
by getting him the help he needed. He
is feeling and looking a lot better
today, and he is also sleeping a lot.
Thanks again.

Included in the letter was a £50 voucher for John Lewis. Our daughter had just turned one and she had recently started walking. People told me she needed some 'cruising shoes', which are softer shoes for new walkers. I used the money to buy her a pair, which I have kept as a reminder of my encounter with Max.

* * *

My daughter is five now, and she is fit and healthy and she talks – a lot. I don't worry as much now as when she was a newborn, though she is clumsy and tends to act before thinking. I worry that she will be a clumsy adult, though hopefully she will grow out of it. One time, she slipped on the living room floor while wearing tights and went headfirst into the doorframe. The cut on her head had to be glued shut (by medics, I might add!) Another time, she decided to take her helmet off while riding her new scooter and went face first into a brick wall. Her eye was swollen shut and the bruise turned all colours of the rainbow. It breaks my heart seeing my daughter hurting, and her knees resemble a hockey player's. But the accidents don't faze her, and she always bounces back as if they've never happened. Meanwhile, the worry bubble above my head grows a little larger each time.

This bubble was massive last year, when Dave and I decided to take our daughter for her first holiday. We thought we would do a weekend to begin with, so we chose Disneyland Paris for her fifth birthday celebration. She was over the moon. At 3am, we got up to get ready for our flight. She put on her Princess Belle dress and grabbed her suitcase. There was no fear and no looking back for her – she had princesses to meet! She was surprisingly chatty for that time in the morning, which I put down to all the excitement. I thought she was bound to fall asleep on the plane. Nope. She was colouring and doing stickers and chatting even more. She did really well on the flight, and I feel lucky that she is so robust and unafraid of stuff. She has always been that way.

When we got off the plane and boarded the magical shuttle bus, she was still really excited, and she showed off her Princess Belle dress to anyone who would look. However, within 10 minutes of us setting off, she was asleep. Boom, she went out like a light. We had to wake her up when the bus pulled up outside our hotel.

After we had checked in, we went to see the park, which was enormous and much bigger than I had expected. My daughter was beside herself; she loved all the Disney music, the toys and the gigantic princess castle in the centre that towered above everything else. We did lots of walking, and we had dinner with the princesses one day and dinner with some other Disney characters the next. It was a little girl's dream come true.

One evening, Dave decided to stay at the hotel, leaving us girls to carry on exploring the park on our own. We were walking back when I accidentally took a wrong turn and got us lost. It was 11 pm by then and pitch black. My daughter was understandably wary, and she kept saying she wanted her daddy, which in translation meant she was scared and Mummy was rubbish. We managed to get to another hotel, where they arranged a taxi for us. I got a bit anxious, as it was dark, and I was in a foreign country with a driver who didn't appear to speak English and seemed to be taking ages to get us back. I thought there might be a chance we were going to be kidnapped, and I only had a bubble wand to protect us. Turns out the taxi driver was just doing his job, and we arrived at our hotel safe and sound. My daughter was very happy to see her daddy.

Note to self: Never go wandering in a foreign country on your own or with your child again. Navigation is not my strong point. I was really scared, as you see so many horror stories on TV, and in that moment, I hoped nothing bad was going to happen to us. Nothing did.

My girl had an amazing time in Disneyland, and when we returned home, my thoughts turned to Christmas. As it was only ever the three of us, going away for the festive period was do-able. Dave and I had enjoyed our first ever holiday in Lanzarote, so we decided to go back there. We'd had such an amazing time, and hopefully our daughter would love it too. So, we left behind the cold and dark of late December and headed to the Canaries, which was enjoying 22-degree sunshine. Yes, that's right, it was 22 degrees. It's true what they say, warmer climes really do put people in a better mood. As soon as the sun hit my face, I felt relaxed, happier and calmer. My daughter had a fantastic time while we were away; she learnt to swim in the pool, saw lots of shows, ate great food, met more people dressed up as Disney characters, made friends at the kids' club and experienced Christmas in another country. My parents never took me on holiday, so the fact I was able to take her to two different countries in one year made me one proud parent.

We didn't take the Christmas presents away with us, as we thought we'd open them when we got home, but the funny thing was, our daughter didn't mention them once. All she wanted to do was play in the pool; it was like Christmas had been put on pause in favour of some even better fun. I am hoping to repeat our sunshine Chrimbo soon.

Alongside writing this book, I am penning one about cats, as I love them so much. As part of my research, I decided to visit a floating cat sanctuary in Amsterdam. And since my daughter and Dave are also feline fans, I took them with me. Unfortunately, we ran out of time, so my girl didn't get to see the floating cats, but she went to a cat museum and had a trip on a canal boat. She also saw lots of cheese shops and had expensive fish and chips, which she fed to the seagulls. Overall, she had a great time. When we got home, I bought her a giant map and we put pins in all the places she has travelled to.

* * *

I love my daughter more than anything in the world, and the things she comes out with crack me up. It's funny how a little human sees the world. Let me give you some examples…

We booked swimming lessons for her, and one day

she announced she didn't want to go to the pool because she was allergic to water.

She once said she saw a black and white worm with legs.

When I taught her about body parts, she couldn't say vagina and said 'jina' instead. *Well, that's close enough*, I thought. One day, my neighbour came over. He and his wife were expecting a baby and he was really excited about it. He asked my daughter if she wanted to meet the baby when it was born. At four years old, this was her reply: "When I was a baby, I came out of my mummy's jina." As if that wasn't embarrassing enough, she then proceeded to point in the direction of said 'jina'.

When we went to Lanzarote, we had just about finished unpacking in our hotel room when I said to my daughter to go and have a wee because we'd be leaving in a minute to get some food. She duly followed my instructions, returning to announce that she wouldn't be needing a drink with her food because she'd already had one from the fountain. Curious, I asked, "What fountain?" Yep, she had drunk from the bidet.

I asked her once how she comes up with all the funny stuff she says, and she replied that she finds it in her head.

I asked her what she wants to be when she grows up, and she replied, "A butterfly superhero." (I have since discovered that what she wants to be when she grows up constantly changes. She has also wanted to be a singer, a ballerina – and a cat.)

When I went to pick her up from school one day, the teacher told me she had been going around kissing all the other children on the mouth. I immediately asked her why she was doing that, but she just smiled sweetly. When we were walking home, I brought it up again, and she explained she was doing it so that all the children could have true love's first kiss.

When she was really little, she said that blue and purple are the same colour, but they just have different names. (She isn't colour blind, we checked.)

When she was three, she told me the peckamaydohs are coming, and then hid under my duvet. I still have no idea what the peckamaydohs are, but if they do come, you heard it here first.

One day, I sent her to her bedroom for 10 minutes of 'time out' as a punishment for being rude. After this time, she came downstairs with nothing on except multiple pairs of knickers. "Look at me, Mummy, I'm wearing 14 pairs of pants!" she said She seemed to have completely forgotten why she had been sent to her room in the first place.

She asked me once if I would like a magazine for my birthday. I replied, "No, thank you, I don't need a magazine." She then said that sometimes people gave her presents she didn't want and that I would get what I was given. Looks like I'm getting a magazine, then!

When she was three, she picked up a snail in the garden and said it was her friend, and that she loved it very much. Then she dropped it, held out her hand and said, "Mummy, it bit me."

Me: "Can you eat your dinner, please.

Her: "No."

"Why not?"

Her: "Because I ate my dinner yesterday."

She had a dummy till she was four and a half, and nothing in the world could separate her from that comfort. At bedtime, she would suck on her dummy and twiddle the canary yellow blanket she had been swaddled in at birth. In a bid to encourage a habit change, as Christmas approached, we asked her if she could put all her dummies in a box and put it under the tree for Santa to take. If she did this, we promised, he would replace them with a special present. She was happy and excited about this, and she even drew a picture of Santa, which she put in the box next to the dummies. She also drew a picture on the outside of the box, just so he would know it was for him. She put it under the tree, and then we put her to bed. A few hours later, she came downstairs and asked for her dummies back. "Santa can keep all my presents," she said. "I don't want any, I just want my dummies." So that was how she got her dummies back, and she also got her presents too. When she was five, she finally gave up the dummy. It was a little sad because she also stopped twiddling the yellow blanket; it's like they went hand in hand. I've kept it just in case she ever wants it back for one last twiddle.

A little cat came into our garden once, and he was wearing a silver bow on his collar. I explained to my daughter he was a boy cat, and she decided to name him Susan.

My daughter was five and a half when she decided she didn't want to wear pull-ups anymore. This was difficult for the first few weeks because she is such a deep sleeper that she would wet the bed without waking up and then feel awful about it. I hated seeing her disappointed face in the morning, and I would encourage her by saying, "It's OK, we can try again tonight." Then I found out about a bed-wetting alarm. Basically, it's a little clip that you attach to the underside of your knickers. A wire goes from the clip all the way up your body, to an alarm that attaches to your arm. Whenever the clip detects moisture, it sets off the alarm, which, hey presto, also vibrates. I showed it to my daughter, and she was on board and wanted to give it a go. So, that evening, I put her to bed with her new device all in place. As the night went on, I had this worried, anxious feeling in my tummy, as I didn't know if the alarm was going to go off. So, I texted my friend and said, "Night one of the bedwetting alarm. It's like waiting for a bomb to go off." Just after I'd pressed send, I thought to myself, *Oh, no, I've just messaged my friend with the word bomb in it. Everyone knows you should never write that word in a text.* Then my brain went into overdrive, and I imagined the bomb squad bursting into my house with guns, shouting at me to get down. Then I pictured them going into my daughter's room and shouting, "She's wired up, the kid is wired up!" Oh my gosh, can you imagine? That would have been awful. Funny but awful.

My daughter said she loves our cat Winter more than me because Winter is prettier. She did follow it up with, "But, Mummy, you do sing exactly like Adele." This is not true, so perhaps she needs her hearing testing.

The moment I sit down for a wee, my daughter will often have this massive need to come in and ask me 20 unnecessary questions and tell me lots of stuff. I said to her once, "Can you just say it through the door?" She replied, "No, I can't say it through the door because I have to see that you're listening."

My daughter was five when I asked her to lay the table for dinner. She didn't respond, so I asked her again. I then said, "Can you hear me? Can you lay the table, please?" She replied, "I heard you all three times, I just didn't want to do it."

One day, she asked me, "What would happen if you went into space with a rocket and then picked a star from space and brought it into the rocket with you?"

My daughter: "What time is it?"

Me: "Nearly 9 o'clock."

My daughter: "So, is it 8 o'clock?"

Me: "No, nearly 9 o'clock."

My daughter: "How many minutes till 9 o'clock?"

Me: "Ten minutes; it's 10 to nine."

My daughter: "Why didn't you say that, then?"

She asked me once at dinner, "Mummy, why isn't spaghetti called noodles?"

Aged eight, we were having Christmas dinner when she looked down at the turkey on her plate and said, "This again? We had *this* last year."

To sum up, being a parent isn't about having all the answers, because I don't think any parent is ready for the random things that children say. I love getting a peek into their world view. At what point did we adults lose that beautiful naivety?

CHAPTER 5

WRITING THE BOOK

D ave suggested I should write a book about my life. He said I had lived more lives than most, and that mine is a story that needs to be told. If anything, he said, it could help people who have been in a similar situation, by showing them that things can turn out OK. It could also educate people who haven't been through this kind of trauma.

I had never thought about writing a book before, and at first, I brushed the suggestion off. But after giving it some thought, I decided there was no harm in at least trying, as it doesn't cost anything to write. So, after dropping my daughter off at preschool one day, I returned home and opened a blank page on my laptop. *Where do I start?* I wondered. *The beginning? The middle?* I stared at my computer screen for a while before deciding to simply document my memories.

All I did was just write what I could remember. I didn't want to fill in the gaps on anything – my mission was to be completely honest – so if I couldn't recollect something, I stopped the chapter there. I wrote what I knew and nothing else. Once I started writing, I couldn't stop, and the memories came flooding back. It felt like I was back in that room where all the bad things happened, reliving them again. It was hard having to go back there and see everything again so clearly, but the words came easy – day and night. My emotions were incredibly raw. It felt like the locked box in my head had been closed for so long that once it had been opened, the secrets I had kept hidden came spilling out. It was as if those words were destined to be written, as if they had a purpose.

The memories pulled me from my sleep, urging me to write them down. In the dark, while Dave slept next to me, I typed out what I needed to on my phone before transferring the words to my laptop the next day. I would spend my day battling the emotions I had stored away, knowing that if I wrote them down and just got them out there, I would then be able to wrestle them back into the box where they belonged. As I said, writing was the easy part. The constant reminder of how broken I was proved harder to deal with. I had to go over each memory several times, returning to the scene and slowing it right down so I could recount all the tiny details. I wanted the reader to see it exactly how it was, frame by frame. The hardest part of writing the book was re-reading what I'd written to make sure I had explained everything adequately. I had to constantly keep in mind that my readers hadn't been present, so I had to give them as much detail as possible or the story wouldn't make sense to them.

The most difficult part was writing about the rape case, as I wasn't emotionally able to go back and relive what happened. But I still wanted to tell the reader about it, and to recount it from my perspective. I started by contacting the Crown Court to find out if I could see the file on the case. This took a long time because I had to go through so many different channels. Seventeen years had passed since the case, so it wasn't as if it was just sitting on someone's desk. When they told me the file was due to be destroyed after 18 years, my mind went into overdrive. If I had put off writing my book for just one year, the file would have been shredded and I would have missed my opportunity to tell my story. Was this destiny? Fate? Who knows. I was informed that as part of the Freedom of Information Act, I could view the whole file under supervision. But because I wanted to share it with the world, I had to wait for a judge to give the say-so on what parts could be published. I waited a really long time for him to do this, and in the end, he only allowed a few documents into the public domain. As it happened, I didn't get to see the entire file in the end, and I'm guessing it has now been destroyed, but I'm grateful for the ones I reprinted in *What Nobody Knew*. Seeing them for the first time was soul-destroying. I only knew my part of what happened, so reading the accounts of everyone else made it feel raw and uncomfortable again.

Now that I had those documents, I thought about trying to get some more. It would be like piecing a puzzle together. To the best of my knowledge, no one had included these types of documents in a book before, and the uniqueness of my quest spurred me on to continue my research into my past.

I put in a Subject Access Request to view my social services file. I had never seen this file before, so I didn't know what to expect. I thought I'd receive it via email, but it arrived in paper form, and there were pages and pages to go through. Although I was pleased to be able to view my case notes, the downside was I found out things about myself I had never been told, which was hard to deal with. But I decided I could either dwell on it or share it and move on. I kept reminding myself that it was in the past. Obviously, I couldn't put all the documents into the book, as they would have filled the entire thing, so I had to filter through them and weave them into the story as I remembered it. Each page became part of the puzzle, and slowly I put it all together.

Many people have asked me if I found writing *What Nobody Knew* cathartic. The answer is no. But publishing it and sending it out into the world was, because it made me feel like I wasn't the only one who went through it.

* * *

While writing my book, I saw a poster on one of the preschool walls about a missing cat. I felt sad for the owners. It's horrible when a pet goes missing, as you worry constantly and imagine the worst. A few days later, my daughter and I went to the park. I sat on a bench while she played on the slide. I noticed a cat nearby just watching us, so I called to her to come and say hello. She ran away, and I thought nothing of it until half an hour later, when she returned and did the same thing. I recognised the cat, but I couldn't place where from. I even questioned whether it was the cat on the poster outside my daughter's school. I racked my brain trying to recall the missing cat's name. It had been clearly written on the poster, but for now it was lost in my head. So, I took a picture of her with my phone. I then tried again to call her over, but she duly darted off.

I told my daughter we were going on an adventure. I showed her the photograph on my phone and said, "Mummy is hoping to match it with the picture on the poster."

We marched to the school. I held up my phone next to the poster and bingo, it was a match! The owner's name was Cherry, and I called her on the number she'd written on the poster. She picked up straight away, and when I explained there'd been a sighting of her cat, she said she would be at the little park in 10 minutes. My daughter and I headed there to meet her. We knew the cat's name now from the poster, so I called it as we walked, but she didn't appear. When Cherry arrived, I showed her the photograph. She was confident that it was her cat, even though she looked a lot skinnier. She went on to tell me that the cat belonged to her late mother, and she had got out and maybe got scared, run off and got lost. We stood together and called for the cat. Cherry had brought some treats with her, and we put them in the alleyway hoping to encourage her out of hiding. While we didn't manage to see her, Cherry left feeling hopeful of her return, and I said I would keep my eye out for her.

Over the next couple of days, I called for the cat whenever I walked past the park, but she never emerged.

Then, four days after we had first spotted the cat, my daughter announced she wanted to go on a bus, as she had never been on one before. So, I took her into town, and we bought some bits before having lunch and catching the bus home. On the way from the bus stop, we walked past the park. We were level with the play area when I saw the cat again. I gently put my shopping bags down in the alleyway, asked my daughter to be really quiet so as not to startle her, and slowly went into the park, softly calling her name. She looked at me sort of confused as to how I knew it, so I repeated it, and with that she came over for a stroke, all the while purring with contentment. I knew Dave was working nearby, so I called him and asked him to nip home and bring a cat carrier to the park. Everything was going to plan until some children came charging by and scared her. Luckily, she only ran just outside the park, and when I called her name, she came back and allowed me to stroke her again.

By the time Dave arrived, I felt I had gained the cat's trust. She let me pick her up and I took her over to the carrier. But all hell broke loose when I went to put her inside it. She didn't want to go in and scratched me and Dave and tried to clamber over my shoulder. I put my hand on the scruff of her neck and gently turned her to the carrier and pushed her in by her bum.

I then phoned Cherry and told her we had her cat; she was overwhelmed with relief and said she would come straight over to my house to collect her.

On the way home, my mind raced. I really hoped this *was* Cherry's cat, because if not I had just stolen someone's treasured pet, and that would take a lot of explaining.

When we got home, we made sure that none of my cats was in the kitchen, shut the kitchen door and let her out of her carrier prison. I then gave her some food and water, which she appeared extremely grateful for. She wasn't scared but she was clearly a little apprehensive. After all, we had just bundled her into a cat carrier against her will. We stroked her and let her sit where she wanted. The doorbell went and Cherry came in. She was beside herself. "Yes, this is definitely my cat," she said. Just to be 100 percent sure, she took her to the vet to have her microchip checked, and her identity was confirmed.

A couple of days later, Cherry invited me round for tea to say thank you. We got chatting and my book came up. I said I was still only at the beginning, but I had written a couple of chapters. I asked Cherry if she minded reading them and seeing if it was worth carrying on. To be honest, I had thought to myself that with all the bad stuff happening in the world, who would want to know about the awful things that had happened to me? I wasn't far off the point of giving up, but Cherry read a bit and said that she really liked it and that I had potential and should continue writing. This was just the boost I needed. Someone actually thought what I had written was worth reading and that I should carry on. So, that's exactly what I did. Thank you, Cherry.

It took me six months to write my book. I would sit at my laptop at the same time every day until it became a habit. There were lots of times when I didn't want to carry on because of self-doubt, and because some of the things I was writing about were just too hard. But I told myself I had come so far already, and gradually the word count grew, which gave me the determination to keep going.

Once I'd finished writing, I had to sort the documents out. I had to blot out people's names to protect their identity. I did this with Tipp-Ex and a Sharpie. Then I found a computer guy who converted the documents ready for inclusion in my book. I didn't want to re-type them, as I wanted them to keep their authenticity, so the reader would know they were reading the real deal. Then I had to check and re-check the writing to make sure there were no mistakes. Finally, I gave it one last read-through to check the story made sense and that it wasn't too confusing. Once the book was ready, I gave it to Cherry to read. She was the first person to read it from beginning to end. She said it made her angry, and it made her cry, but she was very happy with the ending. My hard work had paid off and I had received someone's approval.

Next, I had to find a name for the book. I had a few in mind and two favourites, but I couldn't decide between them, so I spoke to a couple of my closest friends and asked them to pick the one they liked. They each chose a different title, so that didn't really help. Then I decided to throw the net out wider and do a Facebook poll. That way, I'd also be letting all my friends know I had a book coming out.

The choices were:

- *Let Go of What You Know*
- *When Nobody Wants You*
- *It's Just Me Now*
- *What Nobody Knew*

What Nobody Knew quickly rocketed into first place, and I was able to tick 'book title' off the list.

Now it was time to tackle the front cover. As this was a book about trauma and abuse, I wanted to show that monsters are everywhere, but a picture of someone in a box with monsters outside it didn't get a good reception, so I moved onto a different image. This one showed a long, dusty road with a child carrying an oversized teddy. To me, it represented all the baggage she must carry alone. I showed it to a friend, and she pointed out that this type of image is always used for this type of book, and that I needed it to be original and break the cycle. The moment you see a broken child on the cover of a book, you know what the book is going to be about, and my book was about so much more than that. I scrapped that idea and continued my search. After several weeks, I finally found the ideal image. As soon as I saw it, I knew it was perfect. It showed a gavel, representing justice, along with some black birds flying from it, representing freedom. I showed it to my close friends, and they loved it, too. I now had a manuscript, a name and a front cover. I created a blurb for the back of the book, which gave a description of what it was about. Now I was ready to get it published.

All I had to do was send it to some publishers and literary agents.

In total, I sent it to 300 of them. Many of them said they weren't interested, or weren't taking on any new clients, or sorry it's not for us. The rejections came in thick and fast, and I started to doubt myself again. Why did I think I could get a book published when I'd had no prior experience of writing anything before? I had no idea what sort of world I was stepping into.

But what I didn't realise was that I should have had the manuscript professionally copy edited and proofread to make it all shiny and perfect before showing it to publishers. Having failed to do this, it was no real surprise they said no.

Then one publishing company emailed me requesting more chapters. A few days later, they asked to see the full manuscript. I was so happy. I thought they must love the book, and they could see all the hard work and raw emotion I had poured into it.

There is something irritating about waiting. I'm very impatient, so for me it's like a slow torture. I felt like a child who can't wait until Christmas Day to open their presents. I waited three long weeks for them to finish reading my manuscript, only for them to email back to say they weren't going to take it on. However, it was a glowing no, and they told me how brave I was, how much they were in awe of my story, and that I shouldn't give up trying to publish it.

So that was it. Deflated and back to square one, I sent it to a further 150 agents and publishers, this time in Australia, New Zealand, America and Canada. Surely, someone had to take it on. As Angel kept saying, it only takes one to say yes. My mission was to find that one.

That one publisher/agent never came. I felt like I was nothing and that my book was nothing. If people didn't want to take it on, then what was the point? It felt like all my hard work had been for nothing.

Then somewhere along the line, I saw something about self-publishing. This basically involves paying someone to publish your book for you and make it available through all the different sales channels. I got some quotes and went with the company that really seemed to understand the story and could mirror the way I wanted it told. They copy-edited, proofread and typeset the book. The same company helped me to publish it as well. Boom, I was on my way.

On 9th December 2017, my book went up for grabs online. It was on Amazon, Apple Books, Waterstones online, Barnes and Noble online and Book Depository, as well as lots of other places. I was so happy with how things had come full circle. I had set out to write a book, which I had been determined to finish, and I had done it. Now all I had to do was get people to buy it. Surely that couldn't be hard, could it?

I put a post on Facebook saying my book was now available to purchase. If I'm completely honest, I thought I would sell 20 or 30 copies at the most. But then people started buying it and sharing it on their Facebook pages. The support was amazing, so that was a good start. Then I read some very important information online that basically said people are not going to buy your book unless they know about it. This really hit home, and I made it my mission to be heard.

CHAPTER 6
MEDIA

By writing my book, my hope was to make a difference in the world. I wanted to shed light on a range of topics, including domestic abuse, sexual violence, alcoholism, drug abuse, depression and anxiety. These were all subjects that seemed current and relevant, and I wanted to help others garner the strength to either do or say something about their own situation.

I knew marketing was essential, but I was clueless about where to start. First, I set up Facebook and Twitter accounts for the book and ordered 100 copies to hand out free. I then contacted every newspaper I could think of, offering them a chance to review it. Many came back and said they wouldn't do a story on it because I wasn't in their area, and only newspapers in my local area would cover it. I thought that was strange. Wasn't news news regardless of location?

Next, I contacted some radio stations. I emailed them explaining what my book was about, who I was and why I thought it would be a good subject to cover on one of their shows.

Then I googled the fan mail addresses of 50 celebrities

and sent out my book to them, with a little note explaining why I thought they would be interested to read it. I also sent it to lots of different popular TV programmes.

My next task was to get some posters of my book printed up. As soon as they had been delivered, I went from town to town asking shopkeepers if they would display them in their windows. More people said no than yes, but the fact that some people said yes made me feel great.

I received my first response in early January 2018. A reporter from the *Herts Advertiser* said she had received my email and was interested in covering my story. Obviously, I leapt for joy, as I had never been in this situation before and it was incredibly exciting. I had a chat with the reporter on the phone and she asked questions and noted down my replies. She also asked if I had any photos she could run with the article. I duly send her some and waited with bated breath for the article to come out.

Now I had the ball rolling, I decided to record all the ups and downs. Here is a rundown of what happened next, which has been taken from my diary entries at the time.

18TH JANUARY, 2018

I received an email from a lady at BBC Three Counties Radio saying how they would be interested in having me as a guest on their show, and could I send a book for the presenter to read beforehand. I was so excited I immediately took one straight to the post office.

(The Herts Advertiser article was published. It was overwhelming to see my story in a newspaper for the first time. I felt so proud of myself, and I hoped the people who read it would feel the same way.)

The day of my radio interview. The smart building was mostly glass, and when I turned up, I could see all the people working away inside it. My stomach flipped for the millionth time that morning. With Dave in tow, I rang the buzzer. After a short wait in the foyer, a lady came to get us. We sat down with her while she explained what would happen next. In front of her was a room with a big glass window. Above the closed door were the words "ON AIR" in big, red, neon lights.

When the "ON AIR" lights went out, the presenter Nick Coffer emerged from his studio to meet me. I was so nervous I could hear buzzing in my head. Nick said it was lovely to meet me and that it was great of me to come. He said he had read my book and asked me if I was nervous. I said that I really was, and he replied that compared to what I'd been through, which was all documented in my book, this would be a piece of cake. *The man does have a point*, I thought to myself.

He invited me into the studio, and I sat at a desk with a huge microphone in front of me. Nick told me what he thought about *What Nobody Knew*, and the emotions he had experienced while reading it. He explained that all we were going to do was chat about the book, and it would be like I was having a conversation with a mate who asked too many questions. We would then have a break while some music played.

So, off I went. I answered Nick's questions, explaining about some of the topics covered in the book and how I'd got to the stage of publishing it. We stopped while a song played and then went on some more. I was so relieved when it was all over and felt like I'd conquered the world. Nick said that I'd done really well. I asked for a photo with him and then I signed his book. I left the studio feeling on such a high, and when I checked my phone, I saw that lots of my friends had listened to the show and sent messages of praise. Some of the regular listeners also sent me messages through my book's Facebook page. For the rest of the afternoon, I felt like a celebrity, and I went to bed with a huge smile on my face.

8TH FEBRUARY

An interview with the *Welwyn Hatfield Times*. I arrived at their offices and sat down with the reporter, who told me how much she had enjoyed my book. I noticed her taking notes and commented how her words looked like hieroglyphics. She laughed and said it was shorthand. We sat and chatted for a long time while she got her information. I had my picture taken for the article and then I was on my way.

(The story came out the following week.)

19TH MARCH

An interview with Secklow Sounds, a community radio station serving Milton Keynes.

22ND APRIL

An interview with Wycombe Sound, a multi-award-winning local radio station serving High Wycombe and south Buckinghamshire.

I quit my job, handing in my notice after eight years. It wasn't the work I hated but the early starts, which had finally taken their toll. Even though I wasn't doing nights any more, I was still getting up at 3.30 am to start work at 4.30 am. By writing my book, I hoped I could progress in my job and do something else, with better hours. After all, wasn't a published book proof of my additional skillset? Sadly, there weren't any alternative opportunities within the company. So, I had two choices: quit, believe in my first book, write my second and hope they would be a massive success, or continue feeling miserable while listening to my colleagues complaining how miserable they were. You guessed it, I chose the first option. Any normal person would wait until they had another job secured before quitting, but not me. I'm the type of person who gets an idea in their head and runs with it. I don't seem to have the ability to think of the consequences, outcomes and what ifs. It's weird because I live by the motto that if you don't like something change it, but I'm also the first person to say that I don't like change.

Within a single morning, I had decided enough was enough and that I was going to quit my day job and focus on my writing career full time. I didn't tell anyone at work that this is what I intended to do. I didn't want people getting inside my head and trying to change my mind. I had had enough of waking up at 3.30 am, looking at the ceiling and dreading the hours ahead. My decision was final. I went into work and handed in my resignation. As easy as that, it was done. I felt a mix of emotions as I drove home. I felt sad because I had made friends at work, and I was anxious because I had just dragged myself out of my comfort zone, with nothing concrete to move onto. But it was incredible to think that maybe, just maybe, I could be a successful writer. The possibilities seemed endless.

23ᴿᴰ MAY

An interview with SG1 Radio, which serves north Hertfordshire.

27ᵀᴴ MAY

Angel came over and I told her about an idea I'd had to make a promotional video for *What Nobody Knew*. On different pieces of A2 card, I had written the following:

Should a child suffer these:

  Abandonment?
  Domestic abuse?
  Rape?
  Neglect?
  Sexual violence?

Then I'd written:

  As a child
  I suffered every
  Single
  One
  Together we could prevent
  Another child suffering
  This is my story. Read it. Share it. Let's make it stop.

Angel said she'd help me make the video. We decided to

do the filming in a nearby cornfield. This was the plan, and we hoped to do it in one take. I would walk towards Angel, hold up my first card and then toss it away to reveal the next one underneath. After discarding my last card, I would produce my book and show it to the camera. It sounds simple, but we had to do numerous takes, mainly because my daughter, then four, would leap out of the corn and try to catch the pieces of card as I tossed them into the wind. She kept getting into the shot, and we could hear her shouting in the background, "Mummy, Mummy, I've got them!"

(Eventually, we got the video close to how we wanted it and put it on Facebook and Twitter. I thought that 10 to 20 people would see it and, hopefully, share it, too. Oh, how little did I know. The video was shared multiple times and at the time of writing has been viewed more than 50,000 times!)

12TH JUNE

I came up with another ingenious idea to generate some hype surrounding the book. I took 20 copies of *What Nobody Knew* and inside each one placed a sticker that read, "When you have finished reading, please leave for someone else to read. Also, if you are feeling adventurous, please take a picture with you and the book and post it on the *What Nobody Knew* Facebook page #whatnobodyknew. My plan was to leave them on trains and station platforms.

So, I set my alarm for 5 am and headed down to the train station. As I duly set down the copies, I even saw some people picking them up, which made me extremely happy.

16TH JUNE

A lovely lady picked up one of the train books and left this message on the Facebook page: "I have been in London for 10 days, and when I got on the train the other morning, this book was on the seat. I opened it, read a page and thought, *I need to read this*. It took such incredible courage for Amelia to write and relive the horror of her childhood. I know I should leave the book for the next person to read, but I'm not ready to let go of it yet."

(To try and generate some further interest, I decided to set up stalls at fetes and car boot sales. I shifted some copies, and some people took business cards, but I didn't sell as many as I'd hoped to. Here I was standing behind a table and selling my life story, but some people just walked straight past. When that happens more times than people stopping to take a look you begin to doubt yourself. Couldn't people see what a big deal this was to me? Luckily, hope was restored by the people who asked me to sign their book because they had never met an author before.)

12TH JULY

I had a piece published in the national women's magazine, *Take a Break*.

13TH JULY

An interview with Marlow FM.

(In mid-July, I took stock. Despite all my efforts, my book was yet to become a bestseller. The impatient side of me was shouting that all my

hard work had been for nothing, and that I should throw in the towel and be done with it forever. Luckily, the side that told me to keep going shouted even louder. I'd thought that writing the book and self-publishing it was hard enough, but the marketing side was proving harder. There are more than 60 million people in the UK. Surely there had to be more ways of getting my book under their noses? I felt like I'd exhausted all the potential TV programmes, news channels and radio stations. No doubt a lot of them had a list of potential stories to go through before they got to mine. I probably had some waiting to do, but for how long?)

20ᵀᴴ AUGUST

A two-hour radio phone interview with an Australian radio station. I'm going global!

19ᵀᴴ SEPTEMBER

Months have passed since I sent those 50 copies to celebs, news channels and TV programmes, etc., but still there has been no major response. Either people don't care, they are too busy, or they just aren't interested. It makes me feel so deflated. Summer is now over, and with it the potential of doing more outdoor stalls. I don't feel comfortable with the idea of trying to sell my book at Christmas markets. It's hardly a cheery story. I didn't want to be known as "The girl whose book ruined Christmas"!

15ᵀᴴ JANUARY, 2019

I've sent my book to a film director.

21ST FEBRUARY

With book sales stalling, I've decided to start a cat-sitting business, offering to go to people's homes and feed their cats while they are away, check up on them and email the client updates on how they are getting on.

(I thought it would be a great idea to try and get my book on Netflix as a TV series or film. I'd learned that to be taken seriously by the company, you must have an agent to represent you. So, I sent my book off to 50 further industry bods. I wasn't holding my breath, and I realised that these people were probably dealing with more high-profile clients. It made me feel a little sad, because books are constantly being made into films, so I'd imagined it would be an easy ladder to climb. But more than 12 months on, I still hadn't even heard from any of the celebrities I'd sent the book to. I understood that they were extremely busy people and received tons of fan mail, but in my life, I had never tried so hard to achieve something. I'd jumped at any promotional opportunity with both hands. Maybe I'd gone about everything the wrong way and my book would never be a bestseller. Well, at least I could say that I'd tried.)

9TH MAY

I became a member of the Society of Authors, a trade union for professional writers, illustrators and literary translators.

27TH JUNE

An interview with Radio Verulam, which serves Herts. (It has since become Hertfordshire's Mix 92.6.)

. . .

(Reflecting on my journey so far, I hadn't achieved global success with my book, despite trying my hardest. However, I had started writing a new book about cats, and my cat-sitting business was going really well, which meant my schedule was always busy. My main goal now was to get book two and book three written and start the whole publishing process again. I still didn't know where my path was heading or where I'd end up, but that's the fun part of life, isn't it?)

5TH OCTOBER

Being an author is really hard. There are lots of writers out there who want to be noticed, too, and they're all screaming at the world, "My book is unique!" The fact of the matter is that publishers and agents are inundated with people claiming their work is the Next. Big. Thing. I'm still hoping that someone will pick up my book and that it will snowball into a worldwide bestseller, but until that day comes, I'll just have to wait like everyone else. Or maybe it will never happen. The only thing within my control is to keep writing and to never give up.

CHAPTER 7
REVIEWS

The feedback I received for my first book was amazing. I had poured my heart and soul into it without knowing what kind of reception it would get until it was out there. While that was tough, it must have been hard for those reviewers who had been through similar experiences to read my book and write a review, but I feel extremely humbled that they took the time to share their thoughts. It's such a hard subject to talk about, and rather than shy away from it, they were able to relate to my story. I hope reading my book helped them on their journey.

Here is a selection of some of the glowing reviews that make me proud every single day:

Amelia Hendrey is one of the bravest and one of the strongest women I know to share her story in What Nobody Knew. This is her account of the emotional, mental and, most of all, the horrid physical pain that was inflicted on her by her father over and over throughout the years. How her stepmum just let it happen and how her biological mum abandoned her when she was three.

So many times I wanted to jump into the book and rescue her from everything that was going on. You can't help but get emotionally attached to this character, who pulls on so many of your heart strings. In fact, there were two times while reading this book when I literally cried for Amelia. I said this once and I will say it again: nobody deserves what Amelia went through. This is one story that will stick with you way after the book ends.

One aspect of the book that I really enjoyed was the reports from social services. You got their view of what they thought was really happening to Amelia. Obviously, some personal information was left out to protect privacy. However, in this story you got Amelia's truth.

I seriously think this would make an awesome movie on Lifetime TV or a Netflix Original.

I couldn't put this book down. Amelia's story is so deeply moving and challenging, and yet after such suffering, it ends with real hope.

The way she weaves her own experiences with the various agency documents is superb. I found myself thinking of what was happening in my own life on the dates and times Amelia was going through such horrors. This is such an important book. It hits you hard that children are being subjected to horrific abuse and that people around them do nothing for a whole host of reasons. Without directly saying so, it challenges each and every one of us to open our eyes. Amelia, you are an inspiration. A triumph of the human will to survive, and a testament that love overcomes evil.

I never write reviews, but this book was brilliant. As other reviewers have said, once you start reading it, you can't put it down. It's a story of a girl who, in my opinion, and against all odds, dragged herself out of hell… I hope this young woman is proud of her achievements because she should be. I am in awe of her because I don't know if I could survive what she went through.

What an incredible person this author is. To survive a horrendous childhood and to become an intelligent adult able to write with such honesty and clarity is truly amazing.

This is a truly heart-wrenching story. Having picked up the book to read for a while I found myself reading the whole thing. So many things to happen to a child that it's a wonder she came through the other end. A must-read!!!

All of you! Every single one of you! Every nurse and doctor who ever practised should read this! Every 'professional' who has done the Freedom Training and thought we were exaggerating should read this!

Start at page one and don't stop. Read the case notes and see what was written and then compare that with what was actually happening to the child. Then review your own practice and see if you too are colluding with the destruction of a young life.

Incredibly, Amelia survived. She survived being raped and half killed by her father. She survived being dumped in a hostel without any knowledge of how to live. She did not even know what money was. She survived to write this wonderful book, which will not only give heart and hope to thousands of others in her situation but could also encourage those with the power to do so to actually change things.

. . .

A truly amazing real-life story. Once you pick it up, you really can't put it down. I thoroughly recommend it, but be prepared to cry and get angry all at the same time.

This book is a must – an amazing lady. The emotions I felt whilst reading it were frightening. This is real life, and it made my heart melt.

Amazing book. I understood the feeling behind every part of it. Such an incredible inspiration; the pure strength of character! This subject needs to be talked about, and out in the open! Ignoring it is enabling it to continue! THIS IS EVERYONE'S BUSINESS! Do not look the other way! Stop victim blaming! It is never the victim's fault! Amelia, you are incredible!

This is a brilliantly written book that draws you in and makes you want to read it all in one go. Some people may find the subject matter difficult to read, but it is well worth it. Amelia is brave to have bared all and shared her story with the world.

I read this book in one sitting. Could not put it down. Very inspiring to see how no matter what life brings, we have the strength to carry on if we choose to. Well, Amelia proved that.

I have just finished this book. Tbh, I couldn't put it down. So honestly written, and a great read! What an incredible woman!

. . .

This book is a powerfully written, honest and brave account, and it's impossible to put down. I met the author through a wonderful act of kindness on her part. Once I knew her story, I was amazed that she could have had such a terrible childhood and yet become such a caring, giving and generous person. The documentation that is included between the chapters makes it unique and an even more compelling read. Yes, it will make you cry, but it will also leave you feeling uplifted that someone can survive abuse and neglect and become a wonderful mother, wife and a great friend.

Since this is a true story, it is hard to read the things that have happened to this gal. However, this book offers inspiration, hope, love and healing. Kudos to Amelia Hendrey for being so brave to share her life. I read this book in one day. It has a beautiful flow, it is honest, it hasn't been exaggerated and it is poignant. I recommend this book!

The horrible things some children must endure. It saddens me. Amelia's writing style has a way of sucking you into that world. A world where no one in their right mind would want to live. I've read many books about childhood abuse. It is heartbreaking. I have one major rule; I don't give spoilers. However, this is a must-read. And if you are anything like me, you'll be wanting to put your foot up the father and kick the stepmother's tush. That is me being nice. A wonderfully written book by one very brave author. I'll be watching for more of her work.

This story is truly remarkable, inspiring and worth reading. Hearing that somebody could have suffered so extensively without adequate interference from social services – in the UK and only in the 1990s – is shocking and definitely gives food for thought.

I especially liked how the narrative was broken up by the official documents written by the school, police and social services during her childhood. It was interesting to see these legal documents because I have never seen documents of this kind before and, whilst they are tricky to read and not directly linked to the main narrative, they provide an interesting alternate perspective that I have not seen in any other book. Next to the highly personal, emotive and accessible language of Amelia's account, these documents jar and only emphasise her own isolation. A good and effective structural device, I would say.

As I have said, I can hardly believe that Amelia had to suffer so extensively at the hands of her father at such a young age, and her subsequent bravery really is inspiring. Especially seeing that today she is happily married with children, What Nobody Knew captures the power of the human spirit.

We are just blown away by what some people have been through. Amelia has written one of the most candid, raw, heart-wrenching stories we've ever read. She describes her experiences growing up with her disgustingly abusive father and her good-for-nothing, selfish stepmother while all the while knowing her biological mother left her and never looked back. Her writing is so raw and real that while you're reading it, you will feel the breath escape your lungs and the overwhelming feeling of loneliness deep in your being. You will wish you were there to comfort and love her. Reading stories like Amelia's makes me realise time and time again that someone can use their experience for good or for evil. They can make a choice to live opposite their role models or be doomed to repeat their past. It's all so amazing. She painted such a vivid picture of how lonely she was and how unloved she felt. I felt my heart rate accelerate during certain parts, as I just couldn't fathom how any adult, let alone a parent, can be that much of a disgusting piece of ****. Thank God Amelia found it within herself to overcome and move on. I'm so happy she has found love and a purpose in her life!

Poor, poor girl. What a traumatic and horrendous childhood you had!!!! It's devastating to read but beautiful to know you have come out the other side happier, stronger and better!!! Total admiration and respect for you!!! Well done. xx

This book is a totally compelling insight into a life that no child should experience… it gripped me. Couldn't put it down. Great achievement and story of overcoming the odds.

I read this book in one sitting, couldn't put it down. It's a shocking true story, and it makes you feel like it just happened to someone really close. It's written in an easy-to-read style, and it will make you cry.

An amazing read. I could not put this book down. The officials involved should hang their heads in shame. I wish you every happiness for your future.

This book is an incredible true story (including excerpts from various reports) that will have you sobbing – well, it did me!

. . .

I have only just finished reading this book; it made me cry in places and smile in others. This book is so well written, and I can't wait for the next book from Amelia.

This work is quite the departure from the fictional romance I usually read. Oh, how I wish this were a work of fiction! The treatment this child suffered at the hands of those who were supposed to care for her shouldn't happen to the meanest dog, much less to an innocent child. It's appalling the way the system, the school and the community failed her time and again, but sadly, I know this happens to children every day. Although events are stated objectively and leaning towards being downplayed rather than sensationalised, this book deals with very difficult subjects which may be a trigger for some readers.

As I was reading, I found myself asking, "Why?" Why would someone recount the most horrendous events of her life and lay them out for the whole world to read? I imagine the process provided some measure of catharsis and may have helped lay some demons to rest, and I am in awe of the author's bravery and courage. But knowing that horrible things are perpetrated against children every day, I know the author is trying to increase awareness. She went to school, and even the hospital, with suspicious marks and severe injuries multiple times. It's clear the houses in her neighbourhood were close together and the yelling and fighting would have been impossible for neighbours to ignore. Yet no one really intervened. No one questioned and pressed or gave this child any assurance of safety for her to share what happened. We can't afford to close our ears or turn a blind eye if the signs of abuse are right in front of us. A child's life may depend on it.

Many authors would have presented things in such a way as to dramatise and play on the reader's emotions, yet events are given factually, including copies of official documents. Authentic, transparent and realistic, this is a real-life story of physical suffering and emotional abandonment, but also of perseverance, tenacity, amelioration and hope. This book isn't for everyone, but for those who read it, you'll find you have a different frame of reference through which to view your world as a result of sharing this author's experiences.

I don't normally read a lot of nonfiction, but every once in a while, there will be a book that just grabs my attention, calling me to read it. What Nobody Knew is one such book. I may not have any children, but I love children, and books like this one really anger and sadden me. Amelia Hendrey pens a heart-wrenching and devastating true-life account of the suffering inflicted at the hands of a parent.

Amelia, abandoned by her mother when she was three years old, is sent to live with her physically and emotionally abusive father. Her father and stepmother beat Amelia and terrorised her all throughout her childhood. She was neglected and alone for most of her life. Amelia's father was a nasty, nasty alcoholic. He would come home after the pub and beat his own daughter to the point where she had to be hospitalised. Her father threatened her to never tell anyone what he did to her or else she would be sorry. I can't understand how a hospital can see the bruises, her jaw wired shut and just think it was an accident. Why did the hospital not call family services? Why did they just do nothing?

Also, Child Protective Services did get involved and they knew there were issues with Amelia, but still she was sent home with her father time and time again, where the abuse just kept continuing and escalating. Shame on Child Protective Services for NOT doing their job! I know CPS is overworked and underpaid, but this is a child's life you have in your hands. A child that should be nurtured and loved, not abused by a sick parent. This situation should have been fully investigated.

77

The only reprieve Amelia ever received is when she was sent away to a school for emotionally challenged girls. Here, for the first time, she was able to thrive, learn and make a friend. But, when she was sent back home during vacation, Amelia still suffered the abuse from her father.

I can't believe neighbours did not call the police or family services. They obviously knew what was going on. Why did no one step in and help? Why did they just let it continue? Do most people just not care what happens to others anymore? When did people become so heartless?

Personally, I had a very hard time reading Amelia's story, and many times I had to put the book down because I found myself completely frustrated over the lack of help that was offered to her and the complete ignorance of adults who did nothing.

The following is just my personal opinion, and it is an opinion I feel very strongly about. Not many may agree with it either. I believe that a parent who can do this to his/her own child does not deserve to live at all. You should suffer at the hands of another until your life is taken from you. You don't get to eat three square meals a day and watch television in prison. You lost that right the first time you laid your hands on an innocent child. Your life should end immediately. Maybe I am harsh, but I don't think someone who abuses children should be treated like a human being. They are the worst kind of animal ever. Not even an animal… they are a monster.

Amelia Hendrey is an inspiration to adults and other children who have been abused or are still being abused today. She shows us that we should all take a stand. Don't let what happened to her happen to someone else. Amelia is extremely brave to tell her story, and I can see how courageous she is to let us all into her world. Thank you for telling us your story.

. . .

I have wanted to read Amelia's book for a while now, so when she messaged me asking if I would like to review a copy, I jumped at the chance. I knew it would be a hard read, having gone through abuse myself, but it was even more graphic than I expected.

However, I think it's important that Amelia went into so much detail of the violence, as it will open people's eyes to what really happens behind closed doors. Amelia's story is an important one and lays out what it's like to have to keep quiet when you know you'll get hurt if you tell anyone what is really going on.

Domestic abuse is still a taboo topic. I know there are organisations out there spreading the message – I worked for a domestic abuse charity and heard the awful things that people were going through. But we need more coverage out there. One in three women and one in five men experience domestic abuse in their lifetime, and over 750,000 cases of child abuse are reported in the UK each year. We need books like Amelia's to bring to light what happens behind closed doors.

As you can probably tell, I am very passionate about this subject, so receiving a copy of this book was really interesting to me. I've never read anything like it. The closest I've gotten to reading about abuse is in Jacqueline Wilson's Lola Rose, which I adored.

Reading about how Amelia was abandoned by her mum as a child and brought up by an alcoholic, abusive father was scary. I can't imagine how she must have felt. The book mentions suicide because sometimes that feels like the only way out of such a terrifying situation.

I remember reading it and thinking, it can't get worse than this, it just can't. She described her dad beating her, punching her and throwing her down the stairs. I thought it would get better as she went to boarding school, as they couldn't hurt her anymore. But I was wrong. There are, of course, the holidays where you go back home. And that's when it got worse. This part of the book goes into detail about rape and how Amelia had to go to court to send her father to prison. It's such a devastating feeling knowing that rape happens, but when you're reading about it and the repercussions that it has, it is truly heartbreaking and eye-opening.

This book is a must-read and we need more books like this to help people speak up. You don't have to go through it alone. Amelia thought she did. She had no one, and then when she found people willing to help her, there was hope. It's heartbreaking and tragic but there's also a message of hope. Don't give up the fight.

Brilliantly written. Awful life story but could not put it down. I'm so pleased things turned out the way they did. Absolute trooper. Amazing writer, amazing woman.

Fantastic read, couldn't put it down from first page; it was shocking and heartbreaking and I would highly recommend.

This book… WOW!!! I wanted to start writing the review when I was only a couple of chapters in. I've read sad books before, but this was the first book that actually hurt my heart. Not only was I sad, but I was filled with an anger that I wasn't able to do anything with. The ability for anyone to share any type of abuse is a big deal. For someone to be able to write a book about it to share with the world is powerful. It was impossible to put this book down.

This story takes you along the journey of a young child that goes through an abusive life filled with nothing but pain. No hugs, kisses or love of any kind. Even worse is that no one stepped in to help. The book is different as it shows actual documentation (with names blocked out for privacy issues) from various departments, including social services, the school, etc. It seemed they all wanted to ignore what was going on, but I'm not sure why or how they could do that. The excuses that were given included "medical issues", yet there was never any proof of it from a doctor. How could no one look into it? How could they sleep at night not knowing for sure what was going on? I am curious what happened to her dear friends, Emma and Angel.

I can't applaud Amelia enough for writing this book. Hopefully, it will open people's eyes as to how a child is made to feel nothing and how they can live without telling. I was able to identify a little bit with parts of this story. I know that no matter how old you get, whether the person who hurt you is alive or not, the memories will find and haunt you out of the blue. Sometimes, it's easy to push them away. Other times, it's nearly impossible.

Being that this is a true story, I want to say that it really touched my heart. I am so happy Amelia made it through her toughest battles, especially with someone who's supposed to be on your side, and was able to tell her story. This was an amazing read, and I am rooting for you!

If I ever met this author, and she was OK with it, I would give her the biggest hug. God love her for surviving what she did and being brave enough to allow us into such a personal part of her life!

CHAPTER 8

ANGEL

Often, people who have read my first book ask what happened to Angel. Well, you will be glad to know I am still friends with her, and she is still a very important person in my life.

Angel moved to London, where she is working hard. When we were younger, she always said she wanted to move to the Big Smoke, and she did. She likes to travel in her spare time, and she reports back to me about all the beautiful things she has seen and done. She has a strong work ethic and knows what she wants out of life. I'm hoping to go on holiday with her one day. It's on my to-do list because, when we were younger, we did a lot of things together but never went on holiday, so I'd like to go away with her before we both reach 50. Last year, we got a jar, and on separate bits of paper each wrote down 10 things we would like to do before we reach the big 5-0. We didn't tell each other what they were, we just folded up the pieces of paper and put them inside the jar. I wrote a Post-it note on the outside saying, "Do not open until 2033". When that time comes, we will open it and see if we managed to do all the things we wanted to do.

I see Angel about once a month, sometimes more, and we catch up over a cup of tea and usually some nibbles. She is my rock, and we talk about life before, life now, our plans for the future and how far we have come. To think all those years ago we were two young girls in a hostel with no idea where our life was going to take us. We were poor but happy, and we didn't really care about our surroundings. Now we are fully fledged adults and see the world in a completely different way. We complain about money, politics, rising costs, being overworked and how the world is changing around us. If only we had realised how simple things were back then we would have appreciated it more, but we still have each other, and that's the main thing.

When I gave birth to my daughter, Angel was over the moon, and she wrote her a letter asking her if she could be her auntie. She was one of the first people to come and meet her, and you could see the instant love between them.

Angel and I are completely different personality-wise, but we share enough common ground to get on perfectly. I suppose if we met now, we wouldn't be friends, but back in the day, we were young and carefree and able to make memories before life and responsibilities got their claws into us. Angel is the friend that I feel most grounded with. When I come up with crazy ideas, she'll go through the pros and cons, so I get a clear picture of the decision I'm about to make. She is always there to listen to me when I'm not sure where my life is going and that annoying uncertainty spills into my head. I'd like to think that I am there for her, too. She loves me for me, and if I'm being a little bit crazy and oddball then she happily tells me so. We have come so far in all these years, and I'd hate not having her in my life. I know lots of people, but there's only a handful I would call friends, and I proudly put Angel at the top of my friends list. Recently, I texted her about how stressed I was. I said that I was writing two books and was overwhelmed with it all because it involved too much juggling. She texted back saying, "Just take a breath and relax. You will do it all because you have done it before."

That's why I love her so much.

One Christmas, Odeon Cinema ran a competition called 12 Days of Christmas. All you had to do was answer a question for the chance of winning a prize. Well, I entered and won. The prize was two tickets to the Odeon Luxe West End cinema in Leicester Square to see a film of my choice. My travel there and back was covered, along with a hotel for the night. I decided to take Angel, as our birthdays are a month apart and it could be our joint birthday present. She was over the moon about the treat, so we chose our film, *Green Book*, and met up in the city centre. The hotel was really nice, though the hallways all looked the same, so it was easy to get lost. As we walked through London to the cinema, it was its normal buzzy self, which Angel is used to as she sees it every day. It was eight in the evening, and it reminded me of the days when Angel and I were younger and craved this lifestyle. It was a shock to me because I had forgotten how alive London is. I live in the country, and so 90 percent of the time my surroundings are really quiet. The cinema was huge and plush, and we were seated in the 'Royal Box', which Angel thought was specifically aimed at her. The seats were like big, comfy armchairs. They even reclined, and you had a little table that you could put your snacks on. It swung back and forth so you could push it out of the way when you didn't need it. I looked around and there were so many other seats stretching higher and higher behind us. In front of us was a balcony, and when I looked over it, I saw a huge drop and people sitting below us. It was an absolutely amazing experience. Happy birthday to us, and thank you, Odeon.

Most years, I throw a birthday party for my daughter at our house. It's a nice way to spend a day with new and old friends. Her birthday is in the summer, so the sun is usually shining, the children are occupied, and we can stand around chatting, or go and dance. Once, we even had our faces painted. (The inner child broke free that day!)

I look back on the days when my circle of friends was a lot younger, freer and bursting with energy. Nowadays, we may face more trials and tribulations, but we stand and chat like no time has passed. Each of us is older (and maybe a little wiser), and each of us is so very different to the other. It's in these moments when I am proud to count these people as my allies.

As I've said, Angel is my main support network, and she's the person I can turn to in any situation. She was there for my wedding, and she supported me through the joys of parenthood. For the past 20 years, she's also given me some memories to treasure always and kept me laughing. So, I would like to take this opportunity to say thank you to Angel. I hope for another 20 years plus of laughs, love and happiness. And thank you for loving me for who I am, with all my flaws.

Other friendships in my life have come and gone. I call these 'throwaway friendships', and throughout my life, I've experienced them more times than I care to remember. They are different to your core friendships, which are made up of the people you keep in constant contact with and share your birthdays, days out and troubles with. The throwaway friendships may last for years, but then suddenly you are not friends anymore, and for no major reason. Maybe one of you moved away, and you've grown apart, or maybe you've just lost interest in each other. These friendships bother me a lot. Maybe it's because I have some abandonment issues, but I find it hard because you put all that effort into making memories and sharing experiences, only for the friendship to suddenly cease one day when they find a shiny new friend and replace you with that person. It's like your life was good enough for them once, but now they aren't interested anymore.

The sad part is that after spending all those minutes, hours, days and years with that person, you both move on and are happy with the change. It's as if the friendship has served its purpose and run its course, and now you are both happy to carry on as if your times together never happened. You go about your day-to-day business barely thinking about them. Then one day you wake up and say, "Whatever happened to so and so? I remember when we did this and that together. I wonder what they are doing now."

But because so much time has gone by, a kind of awkwardness has set in, and you don't know how to reach out. A simple "Hi, how are you?" doesn't seem to cut it, so you leave it, hoping that destiny will reunite you one day, and things will return to the way they were.

In other cases, you fall out with someone, and the mouth that you fed at your house is the same mouth that talks badly about you behind your back. They say all the things they don't like about you, forgetting to highlight how good you were to them when you were friends.

My conclusion to this chapter is that people are like fireworks, and some of them are dangerous to get too close to. I don't understand why they are like that, and I don't think I ever will. You just have to take a chance on people and hope you choose well.

CHAPTER 9
REINVENTION

After all the awful things that have happened in my life, people often ask me how come I am so normal. Well, I am far from normal, I have just learnt to hide my peculiarities. It took a long time to become who I am now, and it involved oodles of self-control and determination. I didn't want to be seen as a victim – I wanted to be normal like everyone else – but it was so hard when there was this baggage constantly tripping me over. Whenever I met anyone new, they would tell me about themselves, and in return all I had was my awful story. After hearing it, people were either apologetic or they didn't know what to do with the information. I hated telling them because I knew what their reaction would be, but I had nothing else to give. After a while, I decided I didn't want this for the rest of my life, which is where the reinvention came in. I started out taking baby steps. First, I decided to change my name. Choosing your new name is harder than it seems, as it's something that's going to be with you for life. I chose Amelia because it wasn't very popular at the time and seemed a normal name to have. I hoped my new name would signal the dawning of a new me.

For many years, I had to train myself not to succumb to thoughts and memories. I had to learn to let go of them and not allow them to affect me. In the beginning, the stuff I carried around in my head was a burden on my shoulders. I had to master shutting it out. That was incredibly hard at first because I was so angry. I was angry at my family for what they had done to me, and I was angry at myself for not being able to be who I wanted to be. Time helps, and at least I had no deadline for change. I had always been tough, with good survival skills, so now I had to train my brain to survive emotionally. I needed to lock out any unwanted memories and thoughts and move forward to become an even stronger human being. That was tough because trauma-related memories are incredibly resilient. When the sadness takes over, your body weakens, and it feels easier to give in to them. I had to get rid of a lot of blame and hate. Hating people is easy, but then it manifests into a nasty feeling inside. I didn't want to end up bitter. So, my task was to remove one lot of feelings and replace them with more neutral ones. Once I had done that, my next job was pretence. I had to pretend these things didn't happen to me. This was my ultimate coping mechanism, as once you pretend to yourself over and over that these things didn't happen to you, your brain starts to accept it, and it feels like a massive weight has been lifted. Slowly, the memories retreat and the nightmares stop. You are not necessarily fully healed, but you are better. By repeatedly pushing the memories out, you are basically manipulating your brain and telling it it got everything wrong. By replacing the bad memories with good ones, you create the mould of the new person you want to become. Now you can be whoever you need to be – who you should have been from the start – and make the most of the life you have left.

Obviously, I had to undo a lot of the work I'd done on myself to write *What Nobody Knew*, but after a while, I was able to put my brain back into 'manipulation mode', as I call it. It wasn't easy, but it's done now and, hopefully, I will never have to return to those awful memories.

The memories taught me something, though. They taught me how to treat people, especially my own child. My heart flips when she smiles because it means I'm doing my job right.

* * *

I have come a long way in my life, and although I'm OK with who I am, there is still room for improvement. I still have a lot to learn, but that's OK. I have flaws, just the same as everyone else.

I love to live in a dream world. I don't like all the awfulness in the world and try to shut myself off from it, as if creating a protective bubble around me.

I tend to love things deeply. For instance, a 700-page book or a must-see film, a tiny kitten or an oversized jumper. These are a few of the things that make my heart swell. Maybe that's because I didn't have a lot when I was younger, maybe it's because I have a lot of love to give, or maybe it's because I haven't learned to love things a normal amount. Whatever the reason, this is part of who I am.

Films have always meant a lot to me. I like to forget about my own life for a couple of hours and immerse myself in another story. It's sort of like I'm living someone else's life for a while. For me, watching a film is going into my safe space. I like to revisit characters who unknowingly saved my life, just by the things they said or the way they made me feel at the time.

I am also easily crushed. I can be flawed by a throwaway comment, a friendship gone awry, a dead animal in the road, the feeling of failure. Along with the ups and the downs, I overthink and worry all the time. I don't know why I do this. I think it's because if I don't analyse things from every angle, I might be unprepared for what's going to happen next. Sometimes that's helpful and other times not so much.

I rarely cry, as my dad drummed it into me that it is a sign of weakness. I don't project this idea onto my daughter, though. She cries because she can't find her doll, because you didn't do her bunches exactly as she wanted them, or because you put her toys away upside down. I guess she is at that emotional age when everything is make or break.

I get that some people are more emotional than others, but I have known fully grown adults who will cry at anything and everything, or who can even sob on cue. I don't cry because I have nothing to cry about.

Although I have wanted to be normal my whole life, I have learnt along the way that there is *no such thing* as normal. Initially, when people tried to reason with me by saying, "But Amelia, who *is* normal?" I just took it as a throwaway comment. But the more people I meet, the more I realise it's true. People are insecure and scared and people don't want to be judged but are happy to judge others; it's just the way of the world. We all have secrets or things that set us apart. People worry too much, or they overthink or are self-conscious. No one really has it together, no matter what they show on the outside. A friend once told me that everyone is just winging it and learning from other people along the way. Plus, everyone has their own perspective on what normal is, and that is defined by many factors, such as the country and culture you were raised in. An objective form of normality simply doesn't exist.

I worry constantly. I fret about something bad happening to me or Dave. My daughter has no family to fall back on, and besides, who would love her as much as I do? But I remember someone telling me that it's pointless worrying about things you have no control over, and I try and keep that in mind.

I think I have a good sense of humour. I can certainly see the funny side of most things. I need to, because before meeting Dave, I lived such a sheltered life. I even thought Europe was a country. This was mainly because people would say they were going "backpacking through Europe". So, I assumed they were visiting a single country. After Dave and I had been together a few years, I announced I wanted to buy a cow from the local farmer. Firstly, I had no idea how much space they would need. I thought we could put one in the garden, and it could live off our grass. We'd build a hut for it and bingo; we'd have free milk every day! But Dave explained cows require loads of space, have to be treated for pink eye and have their hooves regularly maintained to stop them overgrowing. Who knew there was so much work involved in keeping a cow? Another lesson learned.

People say don't sweat the small stuff, but life is full of small things that can easily grow, so what they should really say is ignore the small things, but if they get big then deal with them then.

Being a mum is funny because when you first become a parent you don't realise there are so many different mum types, or what mum type you will end up becoming. There are the gym mums, the eco mums, the late mums, the young mums, the old mums, the low-profile mums, the fashion mums, the helicopter mums, the gossip mums and the superior mums. In our own way, we're all doing our bit to ensure our children become upstanding members of society.

Some wise friend of mine once told me to take advice from lots of different people and then adapt it to the way you want to parent. As long as your child is happy and healthy you are going in the right direction.

I tend to ramble when I'm nervous and speak without thinking. I do it in situations where I don't feel comfortable, which tends to make the situation more awkward. Let me give you an example…

For years, I had been having my smear test with the same nurse, and this nurse decided to move to another surgery. She informed me that she would be leaving and that a new person would be doing the health check. I don't like change as it sets off my overthinking ways, but it's unwise to put off your smear when it's due, so I duly booked my appointment and off I went to see the new nurse. She introduced herself and said, "So, Amelia, I see that today we are going to be doing your cervical screening." Just to try and break the ice, I replied that normally I let people take me out to dinner before showing them my vagina. My joke went down like a lead balloon. That was the most awkward smear I can ever remember having.

So, as a person, I feel I'm doing OK in life. I reinvented myself and I am trying to fit in as best I can. I think I'm doing all right; life is full of swings and roundabouts anyway, and if you are lucky enough to find your people, it doesn't matter how weird you are because they will love you regardless.

PART TWO

CHAPTER 10
THE WORLD CHANGES

This is how I survived the end of the world.

Just kidding, but it certainly did feel like it. In a short space of time, the whole world got swept up in a viral outbreak that began in China, and normality as we all knew it changed – and not for the better. We all went through this together, but while I was living it, I decided to document it. I kept a diary because this was the first time in my life I had experienced something of this global magnitude. So, the next two chapters show you how I lived through Covid-19, and the information I discovered along the way.

Let's take a look at what happened, or at least what we were told had happened.

The source of the virus is believed to be a wet market in Wuhan, China, which sold both dead and live animals. Such markets pose a heightened risk of viruses jumping from animals to humans because hygiene standards are difficult to maintain. Typically, they are also densely packed, allowing disease to spread from species to species. The animal source of Covid-19 has not yet been identified, but the original host is thought to be bats. Bats weren't sold at the Wuhan market, but they may have infected live animals that were present there. Chinese-based researchers think the pangolin, a scaly otherwise harmless mammal that eats ants, may have spread the virus to humans. One theory is they could have been sold at the wet market illegally, as the pangolin is the most poached and trafficked mammal in the world. The Chinese use the scales to treat conditions such as arthritis and skin problems.

Right, so that is where Covid-19 is meant to have come from; now let's look at the repercussions.

It takes a human two to 14 days to develop symptoms after becoming infected.

The main symptoms of Covid-19 are a high temperature, fever, chills, a new continuous cough and/or shortness of breath and, in some cases, a loss or change to your sense of smell and/or taste. Other symptoms are fatigue, headaches, a sore throat and aches and pains. Some patients have mild symptoms, while others have been known to display no symptoms at all. It can spread via droplets emitted by sneezing, and it can live for 12 hours on metal surfaces and on fabric for six to 12. Washing your hands is paramount, as the virus can live on your hands for five to 10 minutes.

Coronavirus is the name for a family of viruses that can cause a range of respiratory symptoms. While they usually lead to mild symptoms, they can trigger more severe disease, as demonstrated by the emergence of SARS (severe acute respiratory syndrome) and MERS (Middle East Respiratory Syndrome). However, Covid-19 has proved the most dangerous of them all, and it remains an urgent threat throughout most of the world.

This is my record of how I coped with the Covid-19 pandemic, and how it affected my life, as I'm sure it did yours. I have also written how it impacted other countries, just to give you an idea of how fast it spread and the devastation it caused. Let's start from the beginning...

31ST DECEMBER, 2019

China informs the World Health Organisation (WHO) about a cluster of cases of an unknown virus.

7TH JANUARY, 2020

Chinese authorities identify the virus as a new type of coronavirus, later named Covid-19.

11TH JANUARY

The disease claims its first victim – a 61-year-old man from Wuhan.

20TH JANUARY

The first coronavirus case is reported in America.

23RD JANUARY

Wuhan, China, the epicentre of the coronavirus outbreak, goes under an unprecedented lockdown, impacting 11 million residents.

30TH JANUARY

The WHO declares a global health emergency, and 171 deaths worldwide are recorded.

2ND FEBRUARY

A 44-year-old man in the Philippines dies after becoming infected. This is first death reported outside China. By this point, more than 360 people have lost their lives.

7TH FEBRUARY

A doctor who was among the first to raise the alarm over the virus dies.

10TH FEBRUARY

China has 908 confirmed deaths and a total of 40,171 infections.

11TH FEBRUARY

The WHO proposes an official name for the disease – Covid-19.

13TH FEBRUARY

The first case of Covid-19 in London is confirmed, bringing the total UK cases to nine.

14TH FEBRUARY

First European death recorded in France.

15TH FEBRUARY

A total of 1,666 deaths have been recorded worldwide.

23RD FEBRUARY

Italy sees a major surge in cases and many towns go into lockdown.

2ND MARCH

I hear about the virus hitting close to home for the first time. There's a case in a town down the road from me. Someone had gone into a doctor's surgery because they felt unwell, and they later tested positive for COVD-19.

3RD MARCH

There are 51 cases in total in the UK.

4TH MARCH

Today is my birthday. I had a nice time, but sadly the UK now has 85 cases in total.

5TH MARCH

Today I went bowling with my friends for a birthday treat. We were all talking about the news, but none of us was too concerned.

6TH MARCH

The UK now has 116 cases.

8TH MARCH

I went out for an Italian meal with my friends. (Little did I know this would be the last time I would be eating out for a while.)

9TH MARCH

There are 13 cases in Hertfordshire, where I live. People have started panic buying toilet rolls, antibacterial hand soap and antibacterial hand gel. I went to the supermarket and wore winter gloves because I didn't want to touch the trolley or pin pad. There weren't any toilet rolls and the shelves everywhere were starting to empty. Watching people panic buy on the news made me feel uncomfortable. People know something's up, and they are scared, but they are not thinking about others.

- China has recorded 80,735 cases and 3,120 deaths.
- Italy has recorded 9,172 cases and 463 deaths.
- Germany has recorded 1,176 cases and 2 deaths,
- Spain has recorded 1,073 cases and 28 deaths.

10TH MARCH

I had to go and pick up my new glasses. I am hyper aware of what is happening in the world around me, and I didn't want to touch the button to cross the road or the call button for the lift – instead I took the stairs. All these places have been touched multiple times and could harbour germs. At the opticians, I got in, got my glasses and got swiftly out, all while keeping people at a distance. Watching the news this evening,

I saw that Italy's and Spain's numbers are steadily growing. Italy has become the first country to implement a nationwide lockdown. It is the second worst hit country after China. (Several other countries quickly followed suit, including El Salvador, New Zealand, Colombia, Poland and Spain.)

11TH MARCH

There are now 16 cases in Hertfordshire. I have started cleaning my house with Dettol wipes and antibacterial spray. I wiped all the door handles and light switches. There are 456 cases in the UK. The WHO has officially declared the coronavirus outbreak a pandemic, as it has spread to more than 100 countries.

13TH MARCH

My friend messaged me saying she has a really bad cold. Could it be Covid-19? She is asthmatic, so she is high risk. I am so worried about her; I don't want to lose my friend. She said her 'cold' keeps giving her headaches. Her boyfriend went to do the food shopping but found the shelves were bare. In the end, her mum managed to get them a few bits. She says she keeps going hot and cold, but she thinks that's just because she's stressed. She swears blind it's not coronavirus, but whenever we talk on the phone she coughs constantly. I told her to self-isolate for 14 days, stay away from people and drink lots of fluid, and if she has trouble breathing to call an ambulance.

There are now 20 cases in Hertfordshire. I am panicking that my daughter might get it and bring it home. They are saying on the news that while children aren't displaying symptoms, they could be carriers. This whole thing is making me really anxious. Spain has declared a state of emergency.

- Total countries with confirmed cases: 121.
- Total cases confirmed globally: 142,095.
- Total deaths worldwide: 5,373.
- Deaths outside of China: 2,197.

14TH MARCH

All I've got to record today are the latest figures.

- The UK has recorded 1,140 cases and 21 deaths.
- Italy has recorded 17,660 cases and 1,266 deaths.
- The USA has recorded 2,340 cases and 51 deaths.
- Spain has recorded 6,023 cases and 191 deaths.
- Germany has recorded 3,953 cases and 8 deaths.

15TH MARCH

It was my daughter's last kickboxing lesson for a while, as they've been cancelled because of Covid. She won a medal and went out on a positive note. The elderly are being told to stay at home and self-isolate. People continue to panic buy, so the shelves are still empty. The UK has recorded 1,372 cases, and 35 people have died.

16TH MARCH

The UK death toll has reached 53. Social distancing measures are introduced across the country. Everyone is being told to stop non-essential contact with others, and to avoid pubs, clubs and other social venues.

17TH MARCH

Odeon has announced the temporary closure of all their cinemas. I panicked and took my daughter out of school. I read how someone had tested positive for Covid-19 without showing any symptoms. I imagined lots of positive people are going around touching things and unknowingly spreading the virus. Then I thought how some of these people could be at my daughter's school, and through no fault of their own are passing it on to her. I rushed down to the school and asked to take her home, which they allowed.

There are 202,270 Covid-19 cases worldwide. In the UK, there have been 1,950 cases and 71 deaths.

The UK Prime Minister, Boris Johnson, has asked that people social distance by staying at least two metres apart unless they live in the same household. He has also announced schools will close on Friday for all pupils apart from the children of key workers. Key workers are defined as people who can still work to help the country. They include NHS workers, police, paramedics and supermarket workers, etc. France has imposed a lockdown. I was relieved about the school closing because I didn't feel so much of a scaredy cat for taking my girl out of school. I felt like I was being on the ball.

18TH MARCH

All I've got to record today are the latest figures.

- Italy has recorded 31,506 cases and 2,503 deaths.

- Spain has recorded 13,716 cases and 533 deaths.
- Germany has recorded 9,877 cases and 26 deaths.
- USA has recorded 6,524 cases and 116 deaths.
- Belgium has imposed a lockdown.

19TH MARCH

The UK has recorded 3,269 cases and 128 deaths. The PM has told people to stop panic buying. The government has once again announced that schools will close tomorrow. In Italy, the coronavirus death toll has surpassed China. France has recorded over 10,000 coronavirus cases.

20TH MARCH

Boris Johnson says all pubs, clubs, cafes, restaurants and gyms are to close from tomorrow. The government says they will pay 80 percent of wages to all employees across the country who will be furloughed due to the virus. I am scared about Dave getting it and passing it on to me. My daughter could be left with no one. It doesn't bear thinking about. Italy has recorded 627 deaths, the largest single increase since the onset of the outbreak. Deaths have surged past 10,000 globally.

21ST MARCH

I have started wearing disposable plastic gloves when I go to the shops.

22ND MARCH

My daughter and I stay at home together, away from the madness happening outside. I'm just waiting for Dave to join us. I'm so worried because he is still out in the world. He's a plumber and is working for an elderly lady who has no bathroom – he says he can't leave her without any facilities. He will stop working once she is sorted. Cases only seem to be getting higher. I need my husband home safe. I wish my anxiety would give me a break. Hopefully, when he is home, it will ease.

Greece enters lockdown.

23RD MARCH

The UK has recorded 6,650 cases. McDonald's has closed its doors, along with other food chains. Boris Johnson has announced a nationwide lockdown for the next three weeks. You are only permitted to go out for one form of exercise a day or to buy essential food items. Non-essential stores have been mandated to close. People who can have been instructed to work from home. The PM emphasises his point by looking directly into the camera and saying, "You must stay at home."

24TH MARCH

There are now 8,077 cases in the UK, and there have been 424 deaths. The lockdown has been partially lifted in China. New Zealand has entered lockdown, while India has announced a 21-day one.

26TH MARCH

The USA has become the hardest hit by the pandemic, with more than 80,000 confirmed cases. At 8 pm this evening, we all stood united on our front doorsteps, balconies and by open windows to applaud and cheer for our amazing and brave NHS staff, who are courageously and selflessly battling to save as many lives as possible. Prince Charles has tested positive for Covid-19 and is now self-isolating. All my cat-sitting clients have cancelled.

27TH MARCH

Dave finished his bathroom job today. To say I am relieved is an understatement. Boris Johnson has tested positive for coronavirus along with the Health Secretary. The government says self-employed people will get 80 percent of their average monthly profits covered.

30TH MARCH

Total deaths in the UK have now reached 1,235.

We are now doing home schooling. I made up a chart to keep us on track. It goes as follows:

- 8.30-9.30 am – Wake up, get dressed, have breakfast, brush teeth, brush hair
- 10-11 am – Colouring, handwriting
- 11 am-12 pm – Reading and a snack
- 12-1 pm – P.E. and kickboxing
- 1-1.30 pm – Lunch
- 1.30-2.30 pm – Maths, English, money, world map, times tables
- 2.30-3 pm – Reading and a snack

- 3 pm – Free time

31ST MARCH

My local shop has adopted a one in one out system. There is red tape on the floor to show people where to stand so they can social distance correctly, which I found helpful. I wore my blue plastic gloves, and when I got home I washed my products in hot, soapy water. My daughter coloured in a picture for our bin collection people and another for postal workers. Underneath each one she wrote, "Thank you for your service." We then put them out where the workers would see them.

1ST APRIL

Entire sports seasons have been cancelled. There's no F1, no Wimbledon, no end to the Premiership, no boat race, no London Marathon. The Olympics have been postponed until 2021. Concerts, tours, festivals and mass gatherings have all been cancelled, and churches are closed.

While China, where the virus originated, initially had the most cases by far, it has now been overtaken by the USA, which has 203,000. Italy has 110,000 cases and Spain 102,000. Germany, France and the UK are closing in behind. The UK has recorded 29,474 cases and 2,352 deaths.

Today, my daughter and I got some chalk and tried to colour the bricks on our drive in different colours, to make it look like a rainbow. We'd only just got started when our white cat Winter rolled in the chalk and ended up with multi-coloured fur, so we gave up and settled for having a rainbow cat instead. Then we decided to wash her in case she licked the chalk and got ill.

An outdoor music festival I was due to attend in August sent me a message saying because of current events they would be postponing until next year. I could either save my ticket to use in 2021 or get a refund. I had been wanting to attend this festival for a while and would love to go, but I had to ask myself where we will be next year. What if there is another wave of coronavirus? Will I really want to be in groups of people after this? The uncertainty took all the fun away, so with all these dark thoughts buzzing round in my head, I clicked on the form for a refund.

2ND APRIL

Global coronavirus cases surpass one million.

3RD APRIL

A temporary hospital, called NHS Nightingale, has been built in just nine days in east London. It has space for 4,000 beds. It was built with the help of up to 200 soldiers a day, who worked long shifts alongside NHS staff and contractors. It was made to create more space for virus-stricken patients on ventilators. Prince Charles officially opened it at 11 am via video link.

The United States has confirmed 32,000 new cases in one day, setting a new record for the largest jump in daily cases.

4TH APRIL

A virtual Grand National has taken place. UK deaths have hit 3,605. Turkey requires all residents to wear face masks in public. Dubai has imposed a two-week lockdown.

5TH APRIL

At 8 pm, the Queen gave a message of hope to the nation. Boris Johnson was admitted to hospital, which is really worrying and shows that no one is immune. Let's hope he can beat it. A tiger at the Bronx Zoo in New York has tested positive for coronavirus.

6TH APRIL

I decided to do my supermarket shopping online because I am too scared to go out. Hot weather has been forecast for next week, so I can see home schooling going out the window. The PM has been moved to intensive care. This is not looking good, and it makes it all a lot scarier. What if he doesn't make it? What if we all die? The UK has recorded 51,608 cases and 5,413 deaths.

7TH APRIL

Today I saw something that's been circulating on the internet. In 2008, a psychic called Sylvia Browne wrote a book giving her predictions for the future. One of them stated that in 2020, a severe, pneumonia-like illness will spread throughout the globe, attacking the lungs and the bronchial tubes, and resisting all treatments. Even more baffling, she said it would vanish as quickly as it arrived, attack again a decade later and then disappear completely.

I found that so interesting. Sylvia died in 2013 and therefore did not live to see her prediction come true. Can people really predict things this far ahead? It does seem too spot-on to be a wild guess. Why didn't she push harder with her prediction to warn us? Maybe she did and people didn't believe her. I guess we will never know.

I had a video call with Angel. It was nice to see her. She didn't seem too concerned about the virus and was looking forward to the upcoming sunshine. An RAF jet in training flew over my house several times. I had never seen one before. My daughter loved it.

- The UK has recorded 55,242 cases and 5,655 deaths.
- Hertfordshire has 870 recorded cases.
- The USA has recorded 386,104 cases and 12,242 deaths.
- Spain has recorded 140,511 cases and 13,897 deaths.
- Italy has recorded 135,586 cases and 17,127 deaths.
- Japan has declared a state of emergency.
- Germany has recorded 105,604 cases and 1,905 deaths.
- Worldwide cases stand at 1,359,854.
- Worldwide deaths stand at 75,959.
- Worldwide, 293,611 people have recovered from the virus.

The police are administering fines to those breaking lockdown rules. People are going out and having picnics and sunbathing in 20-degree weather. I feel sorry for anyone without a garden; lots of nice weather and nowhere to go. It must be especially difficult for those with children.

Officials in Wuhan, China, have lifted the city-wide lockdown after 76 days. In order to leave the city, they must download a mandatory smartphone app that will indicate they are healthy and have not been in recent contact with anyone infected with the virus.

8TH APRIL

Eleven weeks after Wuhan became the epicentre of the virus, the city has celebrated the end of its lockdown with a party.

In the UK, another 938 people have died, bringing the death toll to 7,097. The Chancellor says the PM is improving and is sitting up in bed and talking to doctors. In total, there are now 60,733 cases in the UK. My daughter asked me if toothpaste is made from Polo sweets. I can see why she would think that.

9TH APRIL

I decided to get my daughter a trampoline for the garden, as her existing one broke last summer. But they were out of stock everywhere. She has also asked for a Nintendo Switch for her birthday in August, so I thought I would get her one and maybe give it to her early. But just like the trampoline, they are out of stock everywhere.

At 8 pm, we clapped again for the NHS. My daughter took out all her instruments, which included a drum, tambourine, microphone and vuvuzela. I was extra proud of her tonight, because although she doesn't fully understand what the NHS has to deal with, she still wants to go the extra mile for them. The PM has been moved out of the intensive care unit and put back on the main ward, which is a huge relief. It makes me think that if he can survive it, there is hope for others. My daughter and I went back to our chalk idea. This time, we decided to create a rainbow by colouring the brick wall outside our house. It looked awesome in the sunshine.

The UK has recorded its highest daily death toll. Tragically, 938 people have lost their lives in just 24 hours.

10TH APRIL

A further 980 people have died from the coronavirus in the UK, which brings our death toll to 8,958. We have surpassed Spain's highest daily total of 961.

On the news, it says the number of people in hospital who have been diagnosed with the virus now totals 19,304. The state of New York alone has the highest number of coronavirus cases of any country in the world, with over 160,000 people infected and more than 7,000 dead from the virus so far.

11TH APRIL

My daughter spoke to her friend on FaceTime today. It was really nice to see them chatting and smiling as they would if they were in the same room. Thank goodness for modern technology.

There have been 917 further deaths in the UK.

Sadly, we lost Ginge today. It was his time, as he was old and showing it. I wasn't allowed to go into the vet's with him. I had to leave the cat carrier outside while they collected him. I waited in the car, and they kept me on the phone while they checked him over. They said it was time for him to be put to sleep. I asked the vet if she could please cuddle him, say goodbye for me, and give him a little kiss on his head, and she said she would. I was heartbroken. Once he had been put to sleep, she brought him out and put the carrier near my car. By then I was in floods of tears. She asked if I could wait until she had gone inside until I got out my car to collect him. Once she was out of sight, I took him out of his carrier and held him tight. He was wrapped in a blanket, and I just held him and cried. I didn't care if he was covered in the virus from being in the vet's, I just wanted to hold him. I loved him so much. R.I.P Ginge.

12TH APRIL

The wet markets have reopened in Wuhan. Boris Johnson was discharged from hospital today, thank goodness. The UK death toll has surpassed 10,000. The weather is incredibly warm, well into the 20s, which is unusual for April. My daughter and I made rocky road for the first time today. We mixed chopped glace cherries, mini marshmallows, chocolate buttons, Maltesers, broken-up digestive biscuits and M&Ms. Then we topped it with 400g of melted Galaxy chocolate. We poured the mixture into a dish lined with greaseproof paper, levelled it off and popped it in the fridge to harden for a few hours. Then we cut it into squares and *voilà*. It tasted amazing, and we will definitely be making more.

14TH APRIL

In the UK, a further 778 people have died in the last 24 hours, and 93,873 have tested positive for the virus. Nearly 20,000 people have been admitted to hospital. I had a big food shop delivered today, and it took me over an hour to wash everything in hot, soapy water. It made me realise how much I took for granted being able to put my shopping away without doing any of this. The virus has made me view everyday tasks in a completely different light.

15TH APRIL

A 106-year-old woman, who is believed to be the UK's oldest patient to recover from coronavirus, has been discharged from hospital.

There have been another 761 deaths in the UK, and 98,476 people have tested positive.

16TH APRIL

The UK lockdown has been extended by at least another three weeks. A further 861 people have died in the UK, taking the death toll past 13,000. A 99-year-old former British Army officer, Captain Tom Moore, has raised £12 million for the NHS after walking 100 laps of his garden.

17TH APRIL

Captain Tom has raised a further £8 million for the NHS.

A further 847 people in the UK have died. I repainted my cats' feeding room today. It was long overdue, and it looks brand-new.

18TH APRIL

There were a further 888 coronavirus deaths in the UK today, meaning the total death toll is now over 15,000. I wish people would stop dying. The numbers are consistently high. 114,217 people are infected. The Queen has asked for there to be no gun salutes to mark her 94th birthday, as it would be inappropriate under the current circumstances. My daughter seemed sad today and I thought it was because she missed Ginge. When I asked her if this was the case, she said, "No, because we have more cats." I reasoned that Ginge was her friend, and she replied, "And now he is my dead friend."

- Germany has recorded 141,968 case and 4,377 deaths.
- France has recorded 147,969 cases and 18,681 deaths.
- Italy has recorded 172,434 cases and 22,745 deaths.
- Spain has recorded 191,726 cases and 20,043 deaths.
- The USA has recorded 710,272 cases and 37,175 deaths.

20TH APRIL

Oil prices in the USA have crashed below zero for the first time in history, as demand for energy has plummeted due to the coronavirus pandemic. On a brighter note, it looks like the death rate in the UK is starting to plateau. Today is the lowest figure in nearly two weeks at 449, taking the death roll to 16,509.

We've got a new paddling pool, which we haven't been able to use because it's been raining. As sunshine is forecast today, we are planning to put it up. My daughter is really excited, as she says it's the size of a swimming pool. With everything that's going on right now in the world, if she wants to think it's a swimming pool, I will let her. We'll have sunshine, water and maybe buy some sand. I'm going to pretend I'm on a tropical island somewhere.

21ST APRIL

Our shopping came today. I scrubbed it all as usual and then made some more rocky road. Dave got a pineapple, cut the top off, scooped out the fruit, poured a drink into it, put the top back on, put a straw in it and gave it to my daughter. She was very impressed.

The daily death toll has risen again, and a further 823 people have lost their life. A UK-produced coronavirus vaccine is to be tested on people from Thursday. Scientists say it has an 80 percent chance of success. It is made from a harmless chimpanzee virus that has been genetically engineered to carry part of the coronavirus. 129,044 are infected with the virus, and a total of 17,337 people have died.

22ND APRIL

Today was another hot day. I did some sunbathing and hung out in the paddling pool with my daughter. A further 763 people have died. The Health Secretary says we are at the peak of the crisis. Total deaths have topped 18,000.

23RD APRIL

It was a beautiful 22 degrees today, so I painted the back of my house. We had hot dogs for dinner. I cut the buns down the side and asked Dave to butter them. Without realising I'd cut them, he sliced them down the front, so they fell apart when we tried to eat them. Who knew we had different bun-cutting styles!

We clapped again for the NHS. People were out banging pots and pans, blowing trumpets, clapping and cheering. It was nice to hear everyone united in their support. There have been another 616 coronavirus-related deaths, bringing the total to 18,738. It's the lowest weekday increase for the last three weeks.

24TH APRIL

Covid-19 tests have become available for frontline workers, key workers and healthcare staff and their families. Demand outstripped supply on the first day.

25TH APRIL

Today, 813 people died of Covid-19, taking the total death toll to 20,319. Captain Tom, the man who walked his garden and raised £20 million for the NHS, has become the oldest person to reach number one in the UK music charts. For his 100th birthday, he did a duet with Michael Ball. They sang 'You'll Never Walk Alone'.

The WHO reports there is still no evidence that people who have recovered from Covid-19 are immune to the disease. So far, over a quarter of the world's coronavirus deaths have occurred in the United States.

26TH APRIL

More sun today. It was 21 degrees, so we had a barbecue. Cue lots of splashing in the pool, laughing and sunbathing. Having fun blocks out the nasty stuff that is happening all over the world. I put home schooling on hold, because while the weather is so glorious, I just want my daughter to have a great time. We can get back to it when it rains. It said on the news that the PM will return to work tomorrow.

There were 413 deaths today; it is the smallest numerical increase since 31st March, when the day's death toll was 381. As it stands, there have been 212,708 deaths worldwide.

27ᵀᴴ APRIL

My daughter asked me to take the stabilisers off her bike. She then wobbled on the grass for half an hour while asking me, "How do I ride my bike?" I said to her she needs to find her balance and did a demonstration. Before long, she was busy riding in little bursts up and down the garden. She then asked if she could take the bike onto the road. I thought, *OK, I'm going to need to take plasters, bandages and a whole first aid kit with us.* How wrong was I. Once she was on the road, she was off, riding as if she'd been doing it for years. I was absolutely gobsmacked and immensely proud. I jogged along behind her, my eyes welling up with the emotion of it all. It was such a beautiful moment as she pedalled away while shouting, "Mum, am I doing it?" I replied that she was, and she added, "I really am, aren't I?" She didn't end up falling and hurting herself; it was a really special day.

There were 366 deaths recorded today, which is lower than yesterday, and a lot lower than the beginning of the month. In total, 21,092 people have died.

It was the PM's first day back and he made a statement. He said that while the UK is beginning to turn the tide in the fight against the virus, it is not the time to relax the nationwide lockdown. It has also been the driest April since 1938.

28ᵀᴴ APRIL

At 11 am, there was a minute's silence for all the NHS workers and key workers who have lost their lives to coronavirus. I stood silently watching the news on my phone. What incredibly sad times.

It rained all day today so home schooling was back on. We got through half of it and then my daughter wanted to go out on her bike and show off her newfound talent. So, that's exactly what we did. In the rain.

In the USA, coronavirus cases have topped one million after doubling in 18 days. So far, 56,400 Americans have died from the virus, an average of about 2,000 a day this month.

Spain has the second highest number of cases, with at least 232,000.

On UK soil, there has been another rise in daily deaths. 586 people have lost their fight, bringing the total death toll to 21,678.

29TH APRIL

There's been more rain today, and it's been colder, too. The PM and his partner welcomed a baby son. It is scary to imagine that if things had gone the other way, and he hadn't survived the virus, he would have missed this moment. It is so frightening when you think of it like that.

There's been more bike riding, washing, shopping – the usual Cinderella duties, plus the jobs we never get round to. It feels weird to have such an empty diary. No cat-sitting, no kickboxing (I got into it in 2019, after taking lessons with my daughter), no school run. It feels like a temporary holiday with added uncertainty. I made rocky road again; it is starting to become a weekly habit. I call it my lockdown luxury.

All care home staff and residents can now be tested for the virus even if they don't have any symptoms.

On the news, a video was used to explain the rate of

infection. When the virus started, the R rate was three, meaning that for every one person infected, a further three would come down with the virus. Now the R rate is much lower, at 0.6, which should result in a decrease in the amount of people becoming infected. The reason the R rate has decreased is because of the lockdown and social distancing, which is why it is important not to come out of lockdown too quickly, and why it needs to be done gradually.

30TH APRIL

Today, 171,253 people tested positive for coronavirus. In total, 26,711 have died. The prime minister says we are past the peak, but we still need to stay at home, so we don't set off another wave of infection.

I went out tonight and clapped for the NHS. It was also Tom Moore's 100th birthday. He was made an honorary colonel and became an honorary member of the England cricket team. The occasion was marked with an RAF flypast.

3RD MAY

All I've got to record today are the latest figures.

- In the UK, 315 people died. In total, 28,446 people have lost their lives.
- Coronavirus cases worldwide: 3,545,197.
- Total recovered: 1,148,830.
- Worldwide deaths: 247,305.
- The USA has recorded 1,177,918 cases and 68,173 deaths.
- Spain has recorded 247,122 cases and 25,264 deaths.

- Italy has recorded 210,717 cases and 28,884 deaths.
- The UK has recorded 186,599 cases and 28,446 deaths.
- France has recorded 168,693 cases and 24,895 deaths.

5TH MAY

The Department of Health has announced a rise of 693 deaths, making the total death toll 29,427. This surpasses Italy's latest official figure of 29,315 deaths. The UK now has the highest number of coronavirus-related deaths in Europe.

So far, there have been 3.6 million confirmed global cases of the virus. The USA is the worst affected country, with New York being the worst hit US state by far, with a death count of 25,000.

I took my daughter out on her bike. She is doing so well on it – I'd say she's a natural. Later, I decided it was time for me to have some fun. I stood with my back to our basketball hoop and tried to get the ball in without looking. Fifty or more tries later, I finally got it in the net and felt like a superstar.

I washed my shopping as soon as it arrived today, but I ended up getting soapy water all over my mushrooms – I didn't realise there were airholes in the top of the box. Lesson learned.

6TH MAY

A further 649 people have died in the UK, taking the total death toll to 30,076.

My daughter went for another bike ride and then we

played in the garden. She wanted to copy me and throw the ball behind her into the net. She managed it seven times throughout the day, clever clogs.

We emptied the paddling pool. As it holds so much water, we were able to water the garden with it and then have a water fight. It was really hot again, so it was great to be able to cool off.

7TH MAY

Guess what? Yep, another bike ride. She has taken to cycling like a duck to water. I still feel proud every time I watch her. It was 22 degrees again, so we spent more time in the garden and I made some rocky road. I am still not tiring of this chocolatey goodness. I added Jelly Tots and honeycomb this time and it still tasted amazing. While following my daughter on her bike, I saw some people I knew. I waved and said hi, and it was a reminder of my old life. I miss being sociable and going places.

Another 539 people died today. The total UK death toll stands at 30,615.

Once again, I clapped for the NHS workers. I am so thankful for them; they are true heroes.

10TH MAY

The PM addressed the nation tonight at 7 pm. He said to avoid public transport if possible and to stay two metres apart from people. Fines will be increased if people do not listen. As from 1st June, if the death rate lowers and the infection rate drops, a phased reopening of shops could happen in July at the earliest. The hospitality industry may also reopen. He also said if there are further outbreaks, the government wouldn't hesitate to put on the brakes.

From 1st June at the earliest, children can gradually return to primary school, beginning with reception, Year 1 and Year 6. A new, five-stage Covid alert level has been set up: one means the disease is no longer present and five is the most critical level. The UK is currently at level four and in a position to move in steps towards level three. The PM stressed that any further relaxation of the lockdown measures is conditional; it all depends on a series of big ifs.

Today, 269 people died, bringing the total death toll to 31,855. It is the lowest daily figure since 29th March, when there were 214 fatalities in a 24-hour period.

I felt incredibly emotional all day. I cried twice, which is really unlike me. I think the severity of everything that's happened over the last two months really hit home, and a build-up of emotions needed to be released. The world has gone crazy, and I can't help worrying what will happen next.

Globally, cases have reached four million.

12TH MAY

Today, 627 people died in the UK, bringing the total death toll to 32,692.

11,605 people are currently in hospital with coronavirus.

There have been 3,403 confirmed cases, making 226,463 confirmed cases in total.

I've been having some problems with my mobile, so I decided to buy a new one. The last time I purchased a new phone was five years ago. Wow, I had not realised how much they had come along in that time. The battery of my old phone had been on the way out for a while. Another job ticked off the to-do list.

The government has announced that the housing

market can start up again, and people are now allowed to move home. Garden centres and other businesses have started to reopen.

13TH MAY

I planted some sunflowers today and made French toast for the very first time. First, I mixed two eggs, one cup of milk, one tablespoon of sugar, some cinnamon, some vanilla extract and some maple syrup. I then soaked the bread in the mixture, melted some butter in a pan and fried the bread. *Voilà*! My daughter said it was the best French toast she had ever tasted. Ah, I do love her.

Today, 494 people died, bringing the total death toll to 33,186.

14TH MAY

A new test that can determine whether you have had coronavirus has been approved for use.

15TH MAY

Last night, I clapped again for the NHS. It seemed quieter and less enthusiastic this time, and it seemed fewer people had come out of their homes, which is a shame because these workers continue to risk their lives for us and it takes us just two minutes out of our non-busy lives to show our appreciation. I also took my daughter to the woods. I saw people had painted some stones with pretty patterns, left them in trees and dotted them around elsewhere for people to find. Later, we went back to the woods and collected lots of plain stones. My daughter painted them and then we took them back to the woods and put them in lots of great places.

I have been adding some bits to my shopping for my neighbour who can't go out, and in return she has been making me curries from scratch and leaving them on my doorstep. It beats having a takeaway, which we haven't indulged in since the lockdown began. I have never tasted such a delicious curry in all my life; it makes my toes curl when I eat it. First point of call when life returns to normal is to go over to her house and get her to teach me how to make it. It's times like these when you really appreciate the things you may not have paused to appreciate before.

I will also be glad when I don't have to wash my shopping anymore; it's the task I least look forward to every week. It's scary to think that the virus could be in your house if you don't wash it off, and that one moment of laziness on my part could contaminate my whole family. It's not worth the risk and not a position I want to be in.

There have been a further 384 deaths in UK. That brings the total to 33,998.

17TH MAY

Another beautiful day. We set up the 'pool' again – it is going to be so hard returning to normality and starting our old routines again. There have been 170 further UK deaths, which is the lowest daily number since 24th March. The total death toll now stands at 34,636.

19TH MAY

China, which has a zero Covid policy, has reported six new coronavirus cases, including one in Wuhan.

Another week of scorching weather. Today, the temperature reached 27 degrees. I've spent the past couple of days sunbathing. I wonder how lockdown would have been if we'd had April showers the whole time. I think it would have driven everyone crazy. We have been really lucky with the sunshine, and I am officially the colour of a cooked Yorkshire pudding. It's strange, as I haven't tired of being at home all the time. I think it's because I watch the news and I hear constantly how lethal catching Covid-19 can be. I know my house is safe, therefore I don't feel bored or eager to go out into the world. Of course, I miss meeting up with my friends, but I don't want to die for socialising, and I want my family to be safe.

- The UK recorded 363 deaths today. The total death toll is now at 35,704.
- Coronavirus cases worldwide: 5,077,169
- Deaths worldwide: 329,062
- Recovered worldwide: 2,018,826.
- Active cases worldwide: 2,729,281

It seems the plan to send some children back to school is going ahead, but I don't want my daughter returning while cases and deaths are still high. I understand that she needs her education, but it is my job to protect her, and that is exactly what I will be doing.

McDonald's has opened some of its restaurants as drive-thru only. There is a limited menu and fewer staff.

21ST MAY

More sunshine today. I managed to do a headstand underwater for the first time ever. I can add it to my list of unnecessary lockdown skills that I will never use again. As it's a Thursday, I went outside and clapped for the NHS in the evening. There were 363 further deaths today, bringing the total to 36,067.

22ND MAY

A total of 3,231,921 tests for coronavirus have been carried out in the UK, including the 14,497 tests carried out yesterday. A further 254,195 people have tested positive, and that is an increase of 3,287 since yesterday. Currently, 9,307 people are in hospital with the virus, which is down 14 percent from 10,781 this time last week. A total of 36,393 people have now died, 351 of those today.

China has reported no new domestic cases.

25TH MAY

There have been a further 128 deaths in the UK today; it seems the death rate is finally going down. Hopefully, this will all be over soon. Tonight, Boris Johnson said that all non-essential retail shops are expected to reopen on 15th June. Could this be our road back to normality?

A total of 353,018 deaths have been recorded worldwide.

28TH MAY

I washed my shopping today and clapped for the NHS. It has been hot again all this week. I washed my car but afterwards questioned why, as it's not as if I'm using it.

A further 377 people died in the UK today, bringing the total to 37,837.

The PM says some schools can reopen from Monday. Groups of six people will be able to meet outside in gardens and other outdoor spaces, as long as they stay two metres apart, which finally means friends and family can start seeing each other again. Boris Johnson urged people to avoid seeing too many households in quick succession. Barbecues are allowed, but everyone needs to remain socially distanced, wash their hands and use "common sense". Also, people shielding for health reasons should continue to do so.

I think tonight was the last night of clapping for the NHS, as they are saying the gesture may have run its course. I am happy to clap until there are no more cases and no more deaths. I feel it is the least I can do.

30TH MAY

There were a further 215 deaths today, bringing the total death toll to 38,376.

2ND JUNE

I checked the local stats today and there are only nine new cases in North Hertfordshire. There have been 75 deaths overall.

We put the pool away as rain is on the way.

A total of 324 deaths were recorded across the whole of

the UK.

Italy has reopened its borders to tourists; France has reopened its beaches, cultural and sporting centres.

3RD JUNE

There were 359 deaths recorded in the UK today, bringing the total to 39,728.

Now that I'm writing this diary practically on a daily basis, I don't think I have watched the news so much in such a short period of time.

The fines for breaking lockdown rules range from £60 to £100.

Spain has extended its state of emergency until 21st June.

4TH JUNE

So far, over five million tests have been carried out for coronavirus in the UK. 1,805 cases were confirmed today, and 281,661 people in total have tested positive. There are currently 7,312 people in hospital in the UK with coronavirus, which is down from 8,558 this time last week. From 15th June, face coverings will be mandatory on public transport.

- A further 176 deaths were recorded in the UK today, bringing the total to 39,904.
- The USA has recorded 1,908,367 cases and 109,350 deaths.
- Brazil has recorded 590,485 cases and 32,688 deaths.
- Russia has recorded 441,108 cases and 5,384 deaths.

- India has recorded 224,500 cases and 6,302 deaths.

We didn't clap for the NHS tonight as the feeling is that people have shown their appreciation and the tradition has run its course. This doesn't feel right to me, as it's not like the pandemic is over. So, at 8 pm, I put my hands together by myself in my kitchen. I personally don't think we should stop clapping until the doctors and nurses no longer have to risk their lives just by going to work every day. I didn't wash my shopping tonight. My brain was freaking out, but my heart told me it was OK.

5TH JUNE

We were eating dinner tonight when all of a sudden, my daughter jumped up, ran from the table and started screaming. Confused, I asked her what was wrong, and she pointed to the floor by her chair leg and said, "Spider, spider." I glanced down and saw a black object. I then remembered we'd had curry the night before and the 'spider' was a rogue raisin that must have fallen on the floor. I started laughing so much the tears were rolling down my cheeks. Dave asked what was funny, and I explained that our daughter had run away from a raisin. Luckily, she saw the funny side and started laughing, too. I said I would put it in the bin and got a baby wipe to scoop it up with. But just as I reached down, legs suddenly shot out from the said raisin's body, and I jumped out of my skin and screamed at the top of my voice. It was a spider after all! Dave remarked how the two females in his life are one of a kind.

A total of 7,080 people remain in UK hospitals battling coronavirus.

357 people have died, bringing the total death toll to 40,261.

As of today, anyone visiting a hospital or outpatients must wear a face covering.

I ordered a face mask today, just in case I need to wear one if I go out.

7TH JUNE

It was raining again today, so I took my daughter on a bike ride so we could both get some fresh air. We also decided to get a McDonald's as a treat. It's been open now for more than two weeks, so I figured if there had been any problems with contamination it would have been reported by now. We drove to the Drive-thru and sat silently in the car enjoying our burgers and fries. Oh, how we had missed our Maccy D's. I have no regrets.

A total of 77 deaths were recorded in the UK today – the lowest since lockdown began. Maybe this is the start of it disappearing. I hope so.

No new deaths were reported in Scotland and Northern Ireland.

The latest daily UK update also showed that a further 1,326 people have tested positive for Covid-19 after 142,123 tests were carried out. So far, around 5.6 million tests have been carried out in total.

China has published a white paper stating how it did not try to conceal the virus.

8TH JUNE

Apparently, when the Spanish flu hit in 1918, it wasn't the first wave that did the most damage but the second one, which I think we are in right now with the coronavirus.

Scientists are saying it may have been in the UK in November/ December 2019, but no one was testing for it because they did not know it was here. A few people I know have said they were really poorly between December and January and had a flu-like illness that they could not seem to shift. Someone told me it was the worst flu they had ever had, and it knocked them for six. Had they been unwittingly caught up in the first wave? And is it doing its rounds again and this time causing even worse symptoms? Who knows.

In London, no deaths have been recorded in the last 24 hours. It's the same in Scotland. In the rest of England, a further 59 deaths have been recorded. Let's hope the whole of the UK can be down to zero soon, too.

New Zealand has lifted all lockdown restrictions and declared the country virus free.

South Africa has seen a rapid increase in coronavirus numbers, recording over 50,000 cases in the past two weeks.

9TH JUNE

A further 286 deaths were recorded in the UK today, which takes the total death toll to 40,883.

I was hoping that because the death rate has seemingly gone down recently, it meant we were finally coming out the other side. I know deaths are usually low at weekends, but I still hoped it was coming to an end. Maybe this won't happen as soon as I thought.

It's Dave's birthday tomorrow. I have got him a cake, and his presents comprise chocolate, alcohol and antibacterial hand gel. Hopefully, it will be his only birthday when antibacterial hand gel is appreciated.

Legoland is set to reopen on 4th July with social distancing in place. Next week, McDonald's is to reopen some restaurants to walk-in customers.

The government confirmed it has scrapped plans for all pupils in England to return to primary school this term prior to the beginning of the summer holidays.

The coronavirus infection rate in the UK is the second highest of any major European country.

Yesterday, we had one new case of COVD-19 in Hertfordshire. Today, there have been 11 new cases.

Zoos in England are to reopen from 15th June. Pubs, bars, restaurants and hairdressers will not be allowed to reopen until 4th July at the earliest.

10TH JUNE

On the news today, former key government advisors said that starting the lockdown a week earlier could have reduced deaths by at least half.

A further 245 deaths were recorded in the UK, taking the total death toll to 41,128.

As of 9 am today, there have been 6,042,622 coronavirus tests carried out and 290,143 people have tested positive.

Retail shops can open on Monday provided they follow Covid guidelines. They have been closed for 82 days.

If progress continues to be made on eradicating the virus, children will return to school in September.

France has recorded a decline in the daily death toll, but there has been a rise in confirmed cases.

11TH JUNE

A further 151 deaths have been recorded in the UK.

To get out of the house, we decided to go for a drive. The skies were grey, and it looked like it might start to rain any minute, but it was warm. We decided to stop at the beach, as it was pretty much empty. We picked a nice stretch of sand that no one else was on, dipped our feet in the sea and collected shells. We only spent an hour at the beach, but it felt special because there was no one else around and we did not have to keep looking over our shoulders to ensure we were keeping our distance. I think my daughter needed that little bit of freedom and normality.

Confirmed coronavirus cases in Russia have surpassed 500,000.

12TH JUNE

There were 202 further deaths recorded in the UK today. Although I have been continuing my solitary clapping, I forgot last night because I was distracted by our trip to the beach. I felt guilty this morning when I remembered, so I did a minute's clapping in the kitchen while I ate breakfast.

In total, 5,607 people are currently in UK hospitals fighting the virus.

13TH JUNE

A further 181 people have died in the UK, bringing the total death toll to 41,662.

14TH JUNE

We went to a shop today because we'd promised my daughter a new doll. We prepared by putting on our masks and plastic gloves. The scariest part of the trip was thinking that some people have the virus but don't have any symptoms; the government has named them the so-called super spreaders. I would be interested to find out why they don't display symptoms. And do some people with normal flu fail to develop symptoms, too, or is this just the case with Covid-19? I am also wondering if there are any people out there who are completely immune to the virus. I probably won't get answers to my questions for a good few years yet.

15TH JUNE

Dave went back to work today. I was worried because it's not as if the virus is no longer around, but he will only be working for a few weeks in a client's house, and he won't be mixing with other people, so, hopefully, he will be safe. I've decided to think positive.

Non-essential shops opened today, and on the news, there was footage of people queuing outside them.

In the UK, a further 38 deaths were recorded. Here's hoping the death rate continues to drop.

16TH JUNE

There are currently 5,254 people in UK hospitals with Covid-19.

A further 233 deaths have been recorded, bringing the total death toll to 41,969.

I saw some of my neighbours today and chatted to them from a distance. It was nice to see them and know they are OK; they seemed in high spirits, which was reassuring.

The total confirmed cases of Covid-19 globally stand at 8,063,488.

The virus has so far reached 188 countries worldwide.

17TH JUNE

A further 184 people have died in the UK, which is disappointing as I thought the numbers were coming down. The total death toll is now 42,153.

China has recorded 53 new cases of coronavirus.

18TH JUNE

Fortunately, the Nightingale Hospital, which was built especially for Covid-19 patients, hasn't needed to be put into use. People are saying a second wave might come in July or October, but if we get a vaccine or use a track and trace system, we may be able to avoid it.

A further 135 deaths were recorded in the UK today, and 5,193 people are currently in hospital fighting the virus.

The government is working on an app that will assist with the test and trace system and pinpoint local outbreaks.

19TH JUNE

Scientists claim that sewage samples show Covid-19 was present in Italy in December 2019. The Italian National Institute of Health looked at 40 sewage samples collected from waste-water treatment plants in northern Italy between October 2019 and February 2020. An analysis discovered samples taken in Milan and Turin on 18th December 2019 showed the presence of Covid-19 more than two weeks before China reported its first cases.

A French study also found that a man was infected with Covid-19 as early as 27th December 2019 – nearly a month before the country confirmed its first cases.

A group from Hong Kong has shown the survival of the virus is significantly altered by temperature and humidity. A preliminary report stated that the virus can survive for 24 hours at 37 degrees Centigrade (98 Fahrenheit) compared with a week at 22 C (71 F) and more than two weeks at 4 C (39 F). The data relates to a solid inanimate surface.

- Coronavirus cases worldwide: 8,734,571
- Deaths worldwide: 461,497
- Recovered worldwide: 4,615,994
- Active cases worldwide: 3,657,080
- The USA has recorded 2,293,646 and 121,369 deaths.
- Brazil has recorded 1,032,913 cases and 48,954 deaths.
- Russia has recorded 569,063 cases and 7,841 deaths.
- India has recorded 395,812 cases and 12,970 deaths.
- The UK has recorded 301,815 cases and 42,461 deaths.
- The UK recorded 173 deaths today.

20TH JUNE

The UK has recorded 128 further deaths.

I went to the market today and, as usual, wore my mask. It was quite busy, and I was surprised that only a few people walking around were wearing a face covering. The people who weren't wearing masks seemed content just going about their business. It made me feel like I'd dreamed the entire virus. I would have thought people would want to protect themselves. I bought a huge watermelon – and a 6ft inflatable unicorn!

21ST JUNE

It's Father's Day. I managed to get Dave a marshmallow slab with a photo of him and our daughter printed on it.

I've decided to record some of the global recovery rates, as I keep writing about deaths and I do not want it to be all doom and gloom.

- In the USA, 973,055 have recovered, and there are 1,235,854 active cases.
- In Brazil, 543,186 have recovered, and there are 476,895 active cases.
- In Russia, 339,711 have recovered, and there are 236,858 active cases.
- In India, 228,504 have recovered, and there are 170,994 active cases.
- Official figures show that Germany's coronavirus R number has rocketed from 1.79 yesterday to 2.88.
- A further 43 deaths were recorded in the UK today, bringing the total death toll to 42,632.

22ND JUNE

15 people died today. Overall, a total of 8,029,757 coronavirus tests have been carried out in the UK, and there have been 305,289 positive cases.

The PM is expected to announce tomorrow that the two-metre social distancing rule is to be halved to one metre in a bid to kick-start the economy and support businesses, particularly the hospitality industry.

23RD JUNE

In an easing of lockdown restrictions, Boris Johnson has confirmed that pubs, restaurants, hairdressers, cinemas, museums, outdoor gyms and hotels will reopen on 4th July. As suspected, the one-metre social distancing rule will be halved from the same date. People from two households will also be able to meet indoors, providing they follow the one-metre social distancing guidelines.

Indoor gyms, swimming pools, spas, nightclubs and bowling alleys will remain closed for the time being, while places of worship will reopen for prayer and services. Weddings will resume with a maximum of 30 guests. Schools are set to reopen in September.

A further 171 deaths were recorded today.

24TH JUNE

Health leaders have warned that the UK must urgently prepare for a second Covid-19 wave following the opening of pubs and restaurants. While the future shape of the pandemic in the UK is hard to predict, the available evidence indicates that local flare-ups are increasingly likely, and a second wave is a real risk.

A further 154 deaths were recorded today, bringing the total death toll to 43,081.

25TH JUNE

A further 149 deaths have been recorded in the UK.

On the news today, an ICU doctor reported having coronavirus symptoms for three months. He had no underlying health conditions and went to the gym regularly. He is part of a group of at least 5,000 people from across the country who are suffering from what is referred to as 'long Covid', where symptoms can last for as long as 14 weeks. Scary stuff.

26TH JUNE

A further 186 deaths have been recorded in the UK.

It was 30 degrees today again. News footage has shown thousands of people flocking to the beach and ignoring the social distancing rules.

Spanish virologists believe they may have found traces of Covid-19 in a sample of wastewater collected in Barcelona in March 2019, nine months before the virus was first identified in China.

UK quarantine rules are set to be revised on Monday, meaning summer holidays to France, Greece and Spain are back on.

27TH JUNE

My regular clients have been phoning asking me to cat-sit over July and August. This is a good sign people are returning to normal. My daughter's school sent an email saying she could go back on 13th July for a week. I'm not ready to let her go. If she got coronavirus, I would never forgive myself after so long being careful.

No new Covid-19 deaths have been recorded in Scotland for the second day running.

100 deaths have been recorded in the UK.

When the toast popped out of the toaster this morning, my daughter said, "Bless you." I think a certain someone has had too much time at home. She also asked if people live in bungalows because they are afraid of heights.

29ᵀᴴ JUNE

A further 25 deaths have been recorded in the UK.

Scotland has recorded zero Covid-19 deaths for the fourth day running.

Me: "It's time for bed."
My daughter: "Not at the moment, I am reading this really interesting journal."
Me: "That's a toy catalogue."

I think she knows it's her birthday soon.

30ᵀᴴ JUNE

A further 155 UK deaths have been recorded.

It was reported on the news that cold or hot weather doesn't kill Covid-19, and the virus can live on plastic or stainless steel for 72 hours.

4ᵀᴴ JULY

I haven't updated my diary for a few days because I have been up to my elbows in paper-mache. My daughter wanted me to make her a giant egg for her seventh birthday in August. So, I got a 36-inch balloon, and made a paper-mache mix using four cups of flour and four cups of water. I then cut some newspaper into strips, which I covered in the sticky mixture and stuck to the balloon. It's time-consuming, as you have to do one layer and wait hours for it to dry and then start with the second layer, wait, and then do the third. I asked my daughter what colour she wanted her egg painted, and of course she chose luminous pink. The idea is that once the egg is painted and finished, we will cut a hole in it, fill it with her birthday presents and then seal it back up. Fingers crossed everything goes to plan.

Pubs were allowed to reopen, and some threw open their doors as early as 6 am. Hairdressing salons opened as well.

Spain has put 200,000 people in Catalonia back into lockdown due to a rise in cases.

Leicester has been put into lockdown until further notice.

5TH JULY

Today marks the 72nd birthday of the NHS. A Spitfire will take to the skies over Cambridgeshire to celebrate the anniversary. The British warplane will fly over various hospitals with the words 'THANK YOU, NHS' etched on the underside of the wings. Today, the whole country is invited to come together at 5 pm to applaud those who have been helping us through the pandemic; not just the NHS and the key workers, but everyone who has volunteered or helped keep services and community networks going.

Thousands of people went to the pub yesterday, with some establishments having to close early because of disruption. On the whole, though, people behaved responsibly.

Globally, the WHO has reported a record rise in coronavirus cases over a 24-hour period. The biggest rise in infections is in the USA, Brazil and India. In the USA, there were a further 53,213 cases reported in the latest 24-hour period, ahead of Brazil (48,105) and India (22,771).

In total, 10.9 million cases have been recorded globally, and 523,011 people have died.

So far, the USA has recorded 2.8 million Covid-19 cases.

7TH JULY

I painted our paper-mache egg today and let it dry before filling it with toys. Yay, it was a success. Much mess was created, but it was so much fun. Another lockdown skill learnt.

The Brazilian president, Jair Bolsonaro, has tested positive for Covid-19.

Following the reopening of the pubs on Saturday, three have alerted their patrons that they have had to shut their doors again after a Covid-19 outbreak.

Melbourne, Australia, is being put back into a strict lockdown after a spike in coronavirus cases. It will be locked down for a total of six weeks to try to prevent a second wave.

- In the UK, a total of 286,349 cases have been recorded. 155 deaths have been recorded today, bringing the total death toll to 44,391.
- The USA has recorded 3,087,675 cases and 133,826 deaths.
- Brazil has recorded 1,668,589 cases and 66,741 deaths.
- India has recorded 743,481 cases and 20,653 deaths.
- Russia has recorded 694,230 cases and 10,494 deaths.

9TH JULY

A further 85 deaths have been recorded in the UK.

Indoor gyms and swimming pools are set to reopen from 25th July. Beauty salons, spas, tattooists and tanning salons can reopen from 13th July, and from 11 July theatres, operas, dance and music shows in England can put on outdoor performances.

12TH JULY

A couple of days ago, I attended a friend's daughter's birthday party. It was held in the garden, where we could socially distance. At some point in the evening, they fired up a clay pot. I had seen these for sale at garden centres and just thought they were plant holders. Clearly, that is not their purpose. I absolutely adore the smell of bonfires, and as soon as I got a whiff of it, I fell instantly in love and wanted to know all about these intriguing clay pots. I discovered they are called chimineas and come in clay and cast iron.

Then we had s'mores. How did I get to the grand age of 37 without knowing about chimineas and s'mores?! What other great things in the world do I not know about?

For those of you who don't know, you create a s'more by smothering chocolate or chocolate spread over two crackers and then placing a toasted marshmallow in the middle of them to create a gooey sandwich. I was genuinely excited about this, and the child in me was bouncing around wanting to have a go.

The next day, I ordered a chiminea online and then went out and bought some giant marshmallows. I love making childhood memories for my daughter and doing the things with her that I never experienced growing up.

13TH JULY

I'm due to start cat-sitting again this week. With a few more clients booked in for late July and August, I'll soon be back to business as usual. I haven't heard when kickboxing is going to be back on. I really miss the fitness side, as I haven't exercised properly through the whole of lockdown, and I have also missed my kickboxing friends.

I had to go out to the shops, and I am still really surprised by the amount of people who don't wear masks. Am I just being overly paranoid?

14TH JULY

Boris Johnson has said that from Friday 24th July, wearing a face covering will be mandatory in shops and supermarkets. The police – not retail staff – will enforce the new rule, and anyone failing to wear a face covering (unless they have an exemption) will be subject to a fine of up to £100, or £50 if paid within 14 days.

In the latest science news, antibodies taken from the blood of llamas could be used to help develop a new treatment for severely ill Covid-19 patients. Scientists found that these antibodies, known as nanobodies due to their small size, can bind tightly to the spike protein of SARS-CoV-2, the virus that causes Covid-19, by blocking it from entering human cells and stopping any infection. The hope is to be able to push the breakthrough on into pre-clinical trials.

16TH JULY

A further 66 deaths were recorded in the UK today, bringing the total death toll to 45,119. It's a relief to see the deaths have dropped from the hundreds. Could the virus be coming to an end? I hope so.

This afternoon, I had a go with the chiminea. I haven't toasted any marshmallows or done s'mores yet – hopefully tomorrow night.

Leicester will remain in a local lockdown for at least two more weeks, but from 24th July, restrictions will be lifted for schools and some shops.

18TH JULY

Today, Dave and I celebrated 19 years together. Our journey started so long ago, and I can't picture my life with anyone else.

To mark the occasion, we fired up the chiminea and toasted marshmallows and made s'mores with our daughter. The gooey treat was so yummy, and we will definitely be doing it again. The icing on the cake – or should I say, the topping on the biscuit – was having Angel over. Coronavirus may have put a dampener on everything, but as we sat there munching on our toasted marshmallows, it was as if no time had passed. Covid-19 can try, I decided, but it won't break our spirit. We laughed, chatted and reminisced, and we discussed what people are calling the 'new normal', and the changes we are making in order to fit in with it. But today was so lovely, it felt like life before the pandemic.

19TH JULY

Boris Johnson has set out an updated roadmap for lifting the remaining national restrictions in England. This includes:

- The reopening of bowling alleys, ice skating rinks, casinos and close-contact beauty treatments from 1st August.
- The restarting of indoor performances, subject to the success of trials.
- The piloting of larger gatherings in venues like sport stadiums, with a view to a wider reopening

in the autumn, and the permitting of wedding receptions for up to 30 people.

- From November, social distancing measures may be eased if Covid cases significantly fall.

India has become the third country in the world to record more than one million cases; epidemiologists say it's likely to be months before the infection rate hits its peak.

Cases in Brazil have surpassed two million. Daily cases have doubled in less than a month, with around 40,000 new cases being recorded per day.

The USA leads the world when it comes to infection rates, after recording 3.7 million Covid-19 cases so far.

In the UK, a further 27 deaths were recorded today.

20TH JULY

I finally went to see my chiropractor, after booking an appointment way before all this madness started. I was greeted at the door by the receptionist, who was holding out some hand sanitiser for me to use. Then my chiropractor, Aksel, came out to greet me. All of us were wearing masks. As we chatted, he washed his hands, put on fresh gloves and a plastic PPE apron. I instantly felt sorry for him. It must be hard cleaning everything and changing your gloves and apron every time someone new comes in. I know I'd quickly find the process irritating, but he did not seem too bothered about it, or at least he kept it well hidden. If this is the new normal, then it's quite sad. After my treatment, I waited while he wiped down everything I had touched, then he held the door open for me, so I would not need to touch it.

I thought about him when I got home, and how day in, day out, he had to wipe down everything after each patient visit; what they had touched, every door handle, every seat, and the table they had lay on. He was clearly doing a job he loved, and I thought what a shame it was that he then had to remember to clean everything to protect both himself and his clients. I hope normality will return for him soon because no one wants that long term. Sadly, it could well be the new normal.

21ST JULY

I downloaded an app called the Covid Symptom Study (now called the Zoe Health Study). Each day, I will use the app to record the state of my health. It only takes a minute, and it will help scientists and health services by identifying how fast the virus is spreading in my area and other parts of the UK. Around four million people have signed up, and all the data is analysed daily and shared with the NHS, though it's not linked to the government's contact-tracing app.

23RD JULY

A further 79 deaths have been recorded in the UK today. From tomorrow, wearing a face covering will be compulsory in shops.

24TH JULY

Boris Johnson said today that he believes Britain will be well on the way to getting past the pandemic by the middle of next year. He stressed that there were still some tough times ahead in keeping the virus under control. He also said there were hard times to come economically. However, I have absolutely no doubt this country will bounce back stronger than ever.

A further 123 deaths were recorded in the UK today.

Dave went to see a client, and while they were chatting in the garden, he noticed she had a chiminea with a plant in the centre of it. She explained that she doesn't use the chiminea anymore, and she thought the plant looked nice in its new home. So, my first theory of what they are used for wasn't so strange after all!

25TH JULY

From today, indoor gyms, swimming pools and leisure centres in England are allowed to reopen.

27TH JULY

It rained all day yesterday and today, so we've been spending most of the time indoors. Temperatures are predicted to rise again at the end of the week.

The UK's chief veterinarian officer confirmed that Covid-19 has been detected in a pet cat. This is the first confirmed case of an animal being infected with the virus in the UK. The government says there is no evidence to suggest that domestic animals can transmit the virus to people. The findings suggest the cat contracted the virus from its owners, who had previously tested positive.

The cat and its owners have made a full recovery.

There have also been sporadic reports of felines coming down with Covid-19 in households that also tested positive for the virus in Hong Kong, Belgium, France, Germany, Switzerland, Spain and the USA.

In the early weeks of the UK's outbreak, worried cat owners crashed a veterinary website following confusion over whether their pets would have to be kept indoors. It was later clarified that only cats from households infected with coronavirus or where their owners were self-isolating should be kept inside.

Following a spike in cases, Hong Kong has banned gatherings of more than two people.

28TH JULY

A further 119 deaths were recorded in the UK today.

29TH JULY

I went to the hairdressers. My stylist was wearing a visor-type mask and gloves, and I kept on my own mask. We chatted while I had my hair done, and I enjoyed the experience as I normally would.

A further 763 new cases were recorded in the UK today, and 83 deaths. This brings the total death toll to 45,961.

It's going to be hot, hot, hot for the next two days, so the 'pool' is all set up ready. I never tire of the sunshine.

Scientists have discovered why coronavirus causes people to lose their sense of smell. Apparently, the virus attacks the cells that provide metabolic and structural support to the sensory neurons as well as certain stem and blood vessel cells. The findings suggest that in most cases, Covid-19 is unlikely to lead to persistent loss of smell, which is known medically as anosmia.

The government believes a second wave will happen in October. Originally, this was thought to come in July.

30TH JULY

Today was super-hot, so we hung out in the 'pool' most of the day. Lately, when I've been driving around, I've noticed a lot of people wearing masks *inside* their cars. I don't understand this. It's annoying wearing a mask at the best of times, so I wonder why people feel the need to wear one while behind the wheel. I know we have to take steps to control the spread, but as soon as I have left a shop and am safely in my car, I take my mask off, as I don't want to wear it a moment longer than I have to. Perhaps I will find someone who wears theirs in their car and quiz them about it. Maybe I'm the one in the wrong!

In the UK, a further 846 people have tested positive for the virus in the past 24 hours, which is up from 763 yesterday. On Tuesday, there were 581 cases.

The government has said today that it has paused releasing new death figures because of a question mark over their accuracy.

31ST JULY

It was 34 degrees today, so, once I had finished my cat-caring work, my daughter and I sat in the living room with the fan on watching films and eating chocolate.

Boris Johnson addressed the nation. He said the plans due to come into force on Saturday to reopen casinos, bowling alleys and skating rinks will not now happen until 15th August at the earliest. In addition, indoor performances will not resume, pilots of larger gatherings in sports venues and conference centres will not take place and wedding receptions of up to 30 people will not be permitted, as had also been planned.

He also announced that rules around face coverings would be extended to make them mandatory in all public indoor settings, such as museums, galleries, cinemas and places of worship. He said this measure would become enforceable in law from 8th August.

This comes after new rules announced overnight saw

separate households banned from meeting indoors in Greater Manchester, east Lancashire and parts of West Yorkshire. This followed the UK recording its highest daily total of Covid-19 cases for more than a month.

In other news, today was officially the hottest day of the year so far. Temperatures hit 37.8C (100F) at Heathrow airport.

4TH AUGUST

I haven't written in my diary for a few days because I've been so busy cat-sitting. I've also been organising my daughter's seventh birthday party. It felt mean not to let her have some friends over, so I've limited it to four. I've hired a bouncy castle with lights and a sound system in it, and I'll put the 'pool' up. Hopefully, they'll have an amazing time.

A study has warned that fully reopening schools in September without an effective test, trace and isolating strategy could result in a second wave of coronavirus that's more than twice the size of the first.

A 'state of disaster' has been declared in the Australian state of Victoria following a rise in people coming down with the virus.

Scientists are investigating whether minks can pass on coronavirus to humans following outbreaks at mink farms in Spain and the Netherlands. Around 90,000 of the animals were slaughtered after it was suspected that more than 90 percent of them had contracted the virus. It is thought that infected workers at the farms passed it on to the minks. Scientists believe it is "plausible" that the minks then passed it back to the staff, and they are now exploring how much of a danger the animals pose.

From next week, new rapid tests that can detect coronavirus in just 90 minutes will start being used in care homes and labs. The tests can pick up regular flu as well as Covid-19. The PM says he wants 500,000 coronavirus tests to be available every day by October, amid fears of possible further waves in the winter. Tests are being carried out at sewage plants across England as the government tries to get a head-start on detecting new outbreaks.

5TH AUGUST

Lockdown is to be reimposed in Aberdeen following a rapid rise in coronavirus cases.

12TH AUGUST

My daughter's birthday was a huge success. In May, I ordered her a trampoline, but I was told the delivery wouldn't be until mid-August. Luckily, it turned up on 7th, just in time for her big day. It took me an hour to try and figure out how to put the lower base part together, and I gave up on the rest. Dave took over and it took him the same amount of time to assemble the rest of it. We also put up a dart board in the garden so the adults could have some fun, too. For a moment, coronavirus was forgotten.

However, I had to draw the line at letting my daughter blow out the candles on her cake, as I thought it might make some of the guests feel uncomfortable. I explained my reasoning to her, and she was completely fine with it and agreed with my decision. I am so lucky to have her, as she definitely has her head screwed on right. When the cake came out, we sang happy birthday, cheered and gave her the hip, hip hoorays, so she still felt special. Then we all got into the 'pool' and one of my friends picked her up and held her above us all while we took a picture. She laughed so much.

The pink balloon was huge, and we filled it with colouring books, teddies, sweets and little toys.

I went to a restaurant last night and all the servers were wearing face visors. Some of the other restaurants had their tables out in the street. Although people were finally out enjoying themselves, you could definitely feel the change in the atmosphere. It didn't feel as relaxed as it would have done before the pandemic.

There has been a coronavirus outbreak in New Zealand following 102 days without any domestic transmission. In response, North Island will be placed into level three restrictions and people will only be allowed to leave their homes for essential journeys.

Meanwhile, the UK has recorded its highest daily number of Covid-19 cases for nearly two months. In the 24 hours up to 9 am on 11th August, a further 1,148 cases of coronavirus were reported. A total of 312,789 cases have been confirmed since the beginning of the pandemic.

The pandemic has tipped the UK into the largest recession on record.

- Coronavirus cases worldwide: 20,559
- Worldwide deaths: 746,744
- Worldwide recovered: 13,472,279
- The USA has recorded 5,307,829 cases and 167,781 deaths.
- Brazil has recorded 3,112,393 cases and 103,099 deaths.
- India has recorded 2,333,166 cases and 46,216 deaths.
- Russia has recorded 902,701 cases and 15,260 deaths.

15TH AUGUST

The household meeting ban in parts of the North West, West Yorkshire, East Lancashire and Leicester has been extended for a week.

Theatres, casinos and bowling alleys are opening today as part of the latest easing of lockdown restrictions in England. The relaxed measures will also mean tattoo studios, beauty salons, spas and hairdressers can offer additional services, including face treatments such as eyebrow threading. Skating rinks can also open.

A coronavirus outbreak at a UK sandwich factory has seen nearly 300 staff test positive.

The PM has announced fines of up to £3,200 for repeatedly not wearing a mask, and fines of up to £10,000 are planned for senseless people who host or organise illegal raves that put lives at risk.

As of 4 am this morning, travellers arriving to the UK from France must quarantine for 14 days due to fears over rising numbers of Covid-19 cases in the country.

More than 1,000 coronavirus cases have been recorded in the UK for the fifth day in a row. Spikes in cases have also been reported in several European countries.

16TH AUGUST

I was thinking today about all the books I sent out to celebrities and talk show hosts. With the whole world locked down, one of them must have read it at least. Maybe my books got put in the bin… maybe they didn't go down well with the recipients. Who knows where they are now? It's such a shame, as I thought the subject was an important one for people to talk about. Maybe one day, *What Nobody Knew* will get the wider recognition it deserves.

Dave and I have been playing darts come rain or shine. Today, we heard thunder while we were playing, then it started to chuck it down. We refused to go inside until our game was finished. Good times.

19TH AUGUST

72 workers have tested positive for coronavirus at a dessert factory.

Leicester's salons and nail bars are allowed to reopen, but the infection rate remains too high for lockdown to be fully lifted.

Ireland has significantly tightened Covid-19 restrictions, creating a list of new rules to try and control the spike in cases.

Australia has ordered 25 million doses of Oxford University's potential Covid-19 vaccine, which, it is hoped, will be ready next year.

Heathrow has unveiled plans for a Covid-19 testing facility to replace current measures, which they hope will lead to the end of the mandatory 14-day quarantine for travellers returning from countries that have been removed from the UK's safe list. Arriving passengers will be able to book coronavirus swab tests and have the results sent to them within seven hours.

22ND AUGUST

The UK's public debt has topped £2 trillion for the first time on record.

Households are to be banned from meeting in Oldham and Blackburn, but both towns have avoided a full local lockdown.

The government's scientific advisory group has said the

R number in the UK has risen to between 0.9 and 1.1, an increase on an estimated range of 0.8 and 1.0 last week, and 0.8 and 0.9 a fortnight ago. This indicates the number of new infections is somewhere between shrinking by 3 percent and growing by 1 percent every day. Experts have stressed the figures are estimates and that there is a high degree of uncertainty around them. It may take between two and three weeks for the changes in the spread of Covid-19 to be reflected in the estimates, due to a time delay between initial infection and the need for hospital care.

The director-general of the World Health Organization has said he hopes the pandemic will be over in two years.

New coronavirus cases have topped 1,000 in Italy for the first time since lockdown eased.

30TH AUGUST

Wow, what a week it's been. I've had lots of work on, which is why I haven't updated my diary sooner. I drove all the way to Wales to view a yellow car I'd had my eye on. I fell in love with it, put my deposit down for delivery and drove straight home again.

I also went out to a restaurant with three of my friends. It was wonderful seeing them and catching up. We shared lots of laughter and it felt like life in pre-pandemic times.

My daughter goes back to school on Thursday. I don't even want to contemplate that right now, because I'll over-think it and work myself up into a state. I want her to go back to school because her education is important and she has missed so much already, but I need her to be safe. The government says the chances of children getting seriously ill are slim, but I don't feel anything is guaranteed when it comes to this virus. I have one job to do for my daughter, and that is to protect her, but how can I do that against an invisible killer? Although most people agree that educating our children is essential, the opening of schools might put some upward pressure on the R rate, which the government will need to respond to. Even with all the information we have now, and even with all the tools at our disposal, we still face a really serious challenge when it comes to the virus for at least the next nine months. I would be surprised if we had a highly effective vaccine in place and ready for mass use in a large percentage of the population before the end of winter, certainly before this side of Christmas, though Chief Medical Officer Chris Whitty has stated there is a reasonable chance we will have vaccines in the period before the winter of 2021/22.

Two people have caught Covid-19 for a second time: one in the Netherlands and the other in Belgium.

Researchers have revealed that a man in Hong Kong has caught coronavirus for a second time, some four and a half months after recovering from his first infection. Scientists said reinfections had been expected, but that is still not good news.

Here in the UK, 17 members of staff and two pupils have tested positive for coronavirus at a school in Dundee, less than two weeks after Scottish schools returned. I am not going to lie, reading this did not help with my anxiety.

The two-metre rule has been declared 'outdated', as sneeze droplets can travel eight metres.

2ND SEPTEMBER

My head is all over the place about my daughter going back to school. I know she needs to socialise again, but I have a bad feeling in my tummy that I cannot shift. I think it's because it is out of my control, and if she catches the virus there is nothing I can do about it. I understand that children with a high temperature will be sent home. Although the risk to her is small, what if she gets it and brings it back with her? What if Dave or I fall seriously ill? What if she gets it and doesn't show any symptoms, and then all of a sudden, we get sick without being prepared for it? I just want my family to be safe. I know I am worrying too much, but I can't help it. The whole world was shut down because of this virus, and I am scared out of my mind because it's very much still out there. My head is not my friend, as I keep replaying every possible scenario over and over. However, I am determined not to show my child how scared I am. I am putting on a happy face for her, as I don't want her to be scared, too.

The lockdown rules are to be tightened around Glasgow after a rise in cases.

- The USA has recorded 6,270,129 cases and 189,251 deaths.
- Brazil has recorded 3,961,502 cases and 122,941 deaths.
- India has recorded 3,826,387 cases and 67,183 deaths.
- Russia has recorded 1,005,000 cases and 17,414 deaths.
- The UK has recorded 338,676 cases and 41,514 deaths.

Today, a total of 10 deaths were recorded in the UK, which is a much lower figure than I have documented on previous days. At last, a glimmer of hope.

3RD SEPTEMBER

I just need to get through the next two days.

I didn't like my daughter going off to school today, but I took a deep breath, put my big-girl pants on and got on with it. While loading her up with her book bag, PE bag and lunchbox, I gave her a giant hug and a kiss. I held her a little longer than I normally would. I wanted to hold her there forever and slow time down to a standstill. I told her to have an amazing day and that I loved her so much and would see her later. It was like her first day of school all over again. I cried all the way home.

According to NHS figures, the weekly number of coronavirus cases in England in late August was the highest since the end of May.

A total of 6,732 new cases were confirmed between 20th August and 26th August. This was an increase of 6 percent on the previous week.

5TH SEPTEMBER

Scotland and France have seen a surge in coronavirus cases in schools, which is all a bit worrying.

France has closed its schools after recording Europe's highest daily infection rate. For the second time in two days, there have been more than 7,000 new infections over a 24-hour period.

Closer to home, I thought teachers would be checking the children's temperature, but this isn't happening. So, how will they know if a child has Covid-19? I must hope for the best and deal with the worst if it happens. This is far from over yet.

Leeds, Middlesbrough, Corby, Kettering and South

Tyneside have been added to the government's coronavirus watchlist after cases spiked.

Some areas previously subject to local lockdown restrictions, including Leicester, parts of Greater Manchester, West Yorkshire and Lancashire, will see them relaxed next week.

6TH SEPTEMBER

A further 2,988 new coronavirus cases have been reported in the UK over a 24-hour period, which is up from 1,813 yesterday. Today's number is the highest daily total since 22nd May, when there were 3,287 cases.

I feel like coronavirus is closing in. In a way, it seems like it's a diluted version, as although a lot more people are getting it, not as many are dying from it, thank goodness. It still doesn't stop me being scared, but then everyone in the world is probably feeling the same way.

7TH SEPTEMBER

India has the second highest number of Covid-19 cases in the world. A total of 90,802 new infections have been registered overnight, taking the total number of cases to 4,204,613.

It has taken just 13 days for India to go from three to four million cases; it took Brazil 25 days and the USA 16 days to make the same leap.

- The USA has recorded 6,276,834 cases and 188,941 deaths.
- India has recorded 4,204,613 cases and 71,642 deaths.

- Brazil has recorded 4,137,521 cases and 126,650 deaths.
- Russia has recorded 1,022,228 cases and 17,768 deaths.

8TH SEPTEMBER

The UK's daily death figure has jumped from three to 30 today, and 2,420 new cases were recorded. People in Bolton have been banned from socialising following a rise in cases.

9TH SEPTEMBER

Social gatherings of more than six people are to be banned in England from Monday. This ban will apply to indoor and outdoor gatherings, including private homes, parks, pubs and restaurants. It is the biggest coronavirus crackdown since lockdown was lifted. First offenders will be fined £100, which will double on each further repeat offence up to £3,200.

The government has a new advertising campaign entitled 'Hands. Face. Space'. It's absolutely critical that people abide by the rules and remember the basics: washing your hands, covering your face, maintaining space from others and getting a test if you have symptoms.

14TH SEPTEMBER

I haven't updated for a while because life has returned to some form of normality. In other words, we can go places and do things we weren't able to do before. Now that I'm seeing people more often, life is full of hand sanitiser, social distancing, bubbles, masks and visors.

Since my last update, there has been a 43 percent

increase in the weekly number of coronavirus cases in England. In the seven days to 2nd September, 9,864 new people tested positive for Covid-19. This is the highest weekly number since the government's test and trace scheme was launched at the end of May.

In England, 3,200 new coronavirus cases have been recorded each day.

The R number for the UK has reached above 1. The last time this happened was in early March. Scientists have said the latest estimate for the R number across the UK is between 1.0 and 1.2.

Households are to be banned from meeting each other in Birmingham, Solihull, and Sandwell.

France confirmed 10,561 new coronaviruses over a 24-hour period, the highest daily total since the pandemic began.

From today, social gatherings of more than six people are now illegal in England.

Israel has become the first country in the world to announce a second national lockdown, which will last for three weeks.

18TH SEPTEMBER

Covid-19 is present in the population at 770 UK schools.

Large parts of the north east are facing tighter lockdown restrictions.

The UK has recorded a further 20 deaths and 3,991 new cases, which is the highest daily total since May.

London's famous New Year's Eve fireworks display has been cancelled due to the virus. It won't feel the same without them. Now it will be three… two… one… silence.

The coronavirus R number has increased to between 1.1 and 1.4.

Latest figures have revealed that an average of 6,000 people in England per day are estimated to be newly infected with coronavirus.

More than half of virus patients suffer persistent fatigue, regardless of the seriousness of their infection. In a recent study, researchers found that 52 percent of the 128 people surveyed reported ongoing tiredness and exhaustion, even 10 weeks after their recovery.

21ST SEPTEMBER

Coronavirus cases have hit a four-month high for the second day in a row.

Angel wants to go to Costa Rica in November for six months. I told her it was crazy and terrible timing, but she has had her heart set on it for a while. She isn't the sort of person to let a global pandemic get in her way! She has visited before and fell in love with the country. I've told her I will be recording the stats to see if it's safe for her to go.

On 15th September, Costa Rica recorded 57,361 cases and 621 deaths. Yesterday, they recorded 63,712 cases and 706 deaths.

Roughly 70,000 people in the UK have Covid-19. The government says that if UK cases double every seven days, there will be 49,000 new cases on 13th October.

Four more areas in Wales are to enter lockdown following a worrying and rapid rise in coronavirus cases.

The UK's Covid-19 alert level is being upgraded from level three to level four.

From Thursday, pubs and restaurants will be forced to shut at 10 pm.

22ND SEPTEMBER

From tomorrow, people in Scotland are banned from visiting other households indoors.

Face masks are now compulsory for staff and customers in bars, restaurants, shops and taxis. Fines for failing to wear a face mask will rise to £200.

The UK has recorded 4,926 new cases, the highest daily figure since 7th May.

23RD SEPTEMBER

The UK has recorded 6,178 new cases and 37 deaths.

This does not look hopeful. While deaths seem low, which is good, it looks like the virus is spreading like wildfire again. Are we ever going to be rid of this?

24TH SEPTEMBER

The government has launched a contract-tracing mobile app that people in England and Wales can use to establish whether they may have been exposed to coronavirus. I downloaded it, and it said my postcode risk level is medium.

Today, the UK has reported 6,634 new cases, the highest daily total ever recorded. Forty more people have lost their life. Despite this record number of cases, the UK is still nowhere near a realistic comparison to the peak of April and May, when researchers have suggested there were more than 100,000 new infections in a day.

25TH SEPTEMBER

More than 103,000 people in England are estimated to have had coronavirus in the week ending 19th September. This figure is almost double the previous week, when it was 59,800. These numbers are for infections recorded in the community and exclude hospitals, care homes and other institutional settings.

London has been added to a national Covid-19 watchlist, as cases have increased. The coronavirus R number has risen across the UK to between 1.2 and 1.5. Last week, it was between 1.1 and 1.4.

29TH SEPTEMBER

- Worldwide, one million people have now died from coronavirus.
- Costa Rica has recorded 73,528 cases and 861 deaths.
- The USA has recorded 7,361,633 cases and 209,808 deaths.
- India has recorded 6,145,291 cases and 96,351 deaths.
- Brazil has recorded 4,748,327 cases and 142,161 deaths.
- Russia has recorded 1,159,573 cases and 20,385 deaths.
- Colombia has recorded 818,203 cases and 25,641 deaths.
- The UK has recorded 7,143 new coronavirus cases, which is the highest daily rise since the start of the outbreak.

30TH SEPTEMBER

The biggest ever rise in new Covid-19 cases has been recorded in the UK – 7,108 in 24 hours – and a further 71 people have died, which is the highest number of daily deaths since 1st July.

1ST OCTOBER

In the UK, a further 6,914 cases have been recorded, and there have been 59 deaths.

2ND OCTOBER

Donald Trump and his wife Melania have both tested positive for coronavirus.

The UK's R number has increased to between 1.3 and 1.6.

Costa Rica has recorded 79,151 cases and 904 deaths. (I'm continuing to monitor the figure for Angel's trip.)

5TH OCTOBER

Before the 'rule of six' came into play, I thought we were coming to the end of the pandemic, so I started organising a Halloween party and booked a bull rodeo for our garden. I knew the kids would not be trick or treating, and I wanted to do something fun for them, so they would not feel like they were missing out. Now the new rule limiting mixing has put the kibosh on our plans. I might as well put the Christmas tree up and call it a year.

On a positive note, in 2021, I got my daughter a ticket to see Paloma Faith – her first ever concert. I am hoping Covid-19 will be long gone by then – it's time to start making memories again. So far, we've had eight months of this madness.

In the UK, 12,594 new cases have been recorded, and there's been a further 19 deaths.

There have been complaints that the new 10 pm closure time for hospitality venues is financially damaging for businesses and is also counterproductive, because it forces people out onto the streets at the same time, resulting in mass gatherings and overcrowding.

Today, I had my flu jab, which was mainly because the symptoms of the flu and Covid-19 are so similar, so if I develop any of them, at least I can rule out flu. Talk about thinking ahead!

6TH OCTOBER

The UK has recorded 14,542 new coronavirus cases in the past 24 hours, which is almost 2,000 more than yesterday. There have been a further 76 deaths, taking the total death toll to 42,445.

7TH OCTOBER

Pubs, restaurants and cafes throughout most of Scotland have been banned from selling alcohol indoors for two weeks from Friday.

The UK has recorded 14,162 new Covid-19 cases.

The cinema chain Odeon is to switch to weekend-only opening at a quarter of its 120 UK sites, as audience figures have been slow to pick up following the lockdown.

8TH OCTOBER

A further 17,540 coronavirus cases have been recorded in the UK today, which is around 3,000 more than yesterday.

9TH OCTOBER

The UK has recorded a further 13,864 coronavirus cases and 87 deaths.

There are currently 3,660 people in hospital with the virus, 436 of whom are receiving ventilation treatment. The daily number of admissions is 597.

With the numbers creeping up, I'm feeling nervous again. I feel like another national lockdown is imminent, although the PM has said this could be avoided by implementing local lockdowns where necessary.

In the US, more than 58,000 new coronavirus cases have been recorded.

10TH OCTOBER

All Cineworld cinemas across the UK and Ireland have been temporarily closed until further notice. I hope these cinema chains don't disappear forever. I love going to the movies.

Since the pandemic began, there have been 575,679 recorded coronavirus cases in the UK.

11TH OCTOBER

In Costa Rica, 87,439 coronavirus cases have been recorded, and there have been 1,076 deaths. Angel is due to fly out on 7th November.

I read today that Covid-19 can remain infectious on surfaces such as banknotes, phone screens and stainless steel for up to 28 days.

The UK has recorded 12,872 more cases and 65 deaths. It marks a slight fall from Saturday, when 15,166 cases and

81 deaths were recorded. The total UK death toll now stands at 42,825.

12TH OCTOBER

A further 13,972 coronavirus cases have been recorded in the UK, and 50 more deaths.

Boris Johnson has announced a three-tier lockdown system: Medium, High and Very High.

- Medium level: covers a significant part of England, and in these areas the rule of six will continue to apply, plus the 10 pm curfew for hospitality venues.
- High level: prevents people from socialising with other households indoors.
- Very high: people will be banned from socialising with other households indoors and in private gardens.

Coronavirus cases have gone up four times in four weeks, and there are presently more patients in UK hospitals with the virus than there was on 23rd March, when the whole country went into lockdown.

14TH OCTOBER

I thought I'd take a look at the global coronavirus picture.

- The USA has recorded 8,094,879 cases and 220,939 deaths.
- India has recorded 7,244,024 cases and 110,686 deaths.

- Brazil has recorded 5,114,823 cases and 151,063 deaths.
- Russia has recorded 1,340,409 cases and 23,205 deaths.
- Spain has recorded 925,341 cases and 33,204 deaths.
- Colombia has recorded 924,098 cases and 28,141 deaths.
- Costa Rica has recorded 90,238 cases and 1,124 deaths.

The UK has recorded a further 19,724 coronavirus cases in 24 hours, which is up by almost 2,500 on yesterday. There have been a further 137 deaths, bringing the total death toll to 43,155. There are currently 4,146 coronavirus patients in hospital in England; 468 of these patients are in ventilation beds, up from 376 a week ago.

In France, night-time lockdowns have been imposed on eight cities for a duration of four weeks, and a state of emergency has been declared.

16TH OCTOBER

In the UK, the R number has edged up to between 1.3 and 1.5.

A further 136 deaths have been announced.

It is estimated that between 43,000 and 74,000 people are becoming infected every day.

18TH OCTOBER

In the UK, a further 16,982 cases have been recorded along with 67 deaths.

Italy has tightened up its rules to try and combat a surge in cases, including introducing a rule of six.

19TH OCTOBER

The Welsh government has announced a 17-day 'firebreak' lockdown. Everyone in the country will be told to stay at home, with pubs, restaurants and non-essential shops among the businesses ordered to close.

Meanwhile, Ireland will go to level five coronavirus restrictions – the most severe level – to try and halt the surge in cases. These new restrictions will be in place until 1st December. Schools are to remain open and elite-level sports will be allowed to continue.

In the UK, 21,000 new coronavirus cases have been recorded.

21ST OCTOBER

I went kickboxing, wore my visor, and had a really good lesson. Three days later, I received an email saying that my instructor had started to feel ill over the weekend and was awaiting the results of a coronavirus test. A further email confirmed it was positive. My panic levels went through the roof, and now I must self-isolate for 14 days. Apparently, people are most infectious two days before they show symptoms, and I saw my instructor a day before he started to feel ill.

I ordered a home test kit – I'm not eligible to go to the test centre because I don't have any symptoms and I'm not a key worker. I've also ordered a blow-up bed and will sleep downstairs and wear a mask whenever Dave and my daughter are in the house. I don't know what else to do.

This is a big mess, and it will be an even bigger mess if my test comes back positive.

I feel fine, but that means nothing with this virus, as it can come on suddenly or lead to no symptoms at all. We shall have to wait and see. I am already being super-careful about what I touch in the house, especially things I know Dave and my daughter will also touch. Can the virus be on your hands even if you don't have symptoms?

22ND OCTOBER

I did a test today. It involved a swab down my throat and the same swab up my nose. What sort of test is this? Who came up with the idea? Why can't we just pee on it? This is gross. Anyway, I sent it away, and I should get the results in two days. I can't bear thinking about the test coming back positive. Where will I live? What if I've already infected Dave and my daughter? Thinking about the what ifs is such a mental headache. I've also been trying to remember who I've come into contact with since the kickboxing session. I just want everyone to be OK.

With the virus now so close to home, the latest Covid-19 figures are no surprise. The UK has set a new record for daily coronavirus cases, with 26,688 new reported infections and a further 191 deaths, taking the total death toll to 44,158.

23RD OCTOBER

I still feel scared, and I'm checking my email constantly for the results. A couple of other people who were at kickboxing that night have already done their tests, which have come back negative. I am worried for myself and for the people I have been in contact with. If my results come back positive, they will have to self-isolate for 14 days and then get a test if they show symptoms. It's a giant snowball effect. Sleeping in the living room is no fun, and wearing my mask around the house isn't glamorous, either. I'm only using the shower once everyone else has used it, and I'm even eating at different times from the others because, obviously, I have to take my mask off to eat. I'm continuously wiping down everything I have touched in the house, including the door handles. It seems a little over the top, but maybe it will prevent Dave or my daughter coming down with the virus.

It has now been seven days since I went to kickboxing.

Here is what I have read regarding the incubation period of Covid-19.

- The median incubation period (half of all cases occur before this time and half after) is 5.1 days.
- 97.5 percent of people who develop symptoms will get them within 11.5 days.

So far, I feel the same as normal, but I have to keep reminding myself I could be asymptomatic – producing or showing no symptoms.

It's like I'm in a potentially contaminated bubble. I cannot touch anything or talk to anyone until my test results arrive.

I read online there are three potential results: positive, negative and inconclusive. What if it comes back inconclusive? What does that mean? Will I have to test again? I guess I need to stop panicking and just wait. Dave is extremely calm. His attitude is don't think about it until you have a yes or a no, then deal with it. My translation of that is wait until you're dying and then panic.

I can't help overthinking it. After all, a positive diagnosis could be life changing. So many people's lives have been affected already. As the day went on, I developed a tickly cough and really freaked out. I hope this isn't the start of my symptoms.

24TH OCTOBER

I woke up with the tickly cough again. Then at 8 am, my test results came through. The email read, "We could not read your coronavirus test sample; this means it is not possible to say if you had the virus when the test was done."

Aaaaagh!

Dave has been coughing this week, too, but he swears it's not Covid. I'm not taking any chances, so we booked in at a test centre for 10.30 am. We drove up in the car, showed the codes we had been emailed and were handed kits to do the test with. We read the instructions and did the swab. Afterwards, we had to drive to another area to drop them off. Dave couldn't drive with all the paperwork and test stuff on his lap, so I took everything off him, put the paperwork on the floor and put his test on my lap next to mine. When we got to the specified area, the man requested Dave's test first. Looking down at my lap, I realised I had no idea which was which. I began to panic and could feel pins and needles in my face. In the end, I just picked the one nearest to the man and said, "This one." When he asked for mine, I handed over the other one and hoped for the best. On the way home, I reasoned that if they both came back negative all will be fine, and if they both came back positive that will be unfortunate, but still fine. However, if one comes back negative and the other positive, we are not going to know who has Covid. What a mess.

For now, it's a waiting game… again. I didn't sleep while waiting for the first set of results, and the whole charade is becoming emotionally draining. My daughter slept on the air mattress with me last night; she said she didn't care if I had coronavirus, she just wanted to lay with me and be close. I love her so much; she has a beautiful heart.

Just a thought. With reports of people getting coronavirus twice, are they actually getting it for the second time or could it be long Covid?

In the UK, a further 23,012 coronavirus cases have been reported, and 174 deaths.

25TH OCTOBER

Dave thinks there will be another lockdown. With that in mind, we decided to buy a pool table. That way, if we are forced to stay indoors again, at least we will have a pool table and darts to keep us occupied.

The wait for the test results is driving me mad; the not knowing is excruciating. I am now 90 percent sure I do not have the virus, but like in a film or a book, there's always the possibility of a plot twist you never saw coming.

In the UK, a further 19,790 coronavirus cases have been reported, and 151 deaths.

26TH OCTOBER

Still waiting.

It feels like forever has passed, and I am still unable to see anyone or go anywhere. Just tell me already!

In the UK, a further 20,890 new coronavirus cases have been reported, and 102 deaths. It's scary to think how fast this virus is spreading. Twenty thousand is a lot of people.

Boots plans to roll out a new coronavirus testing service that can deliver results in just 12 minutes. The swab tests will cost £120 and are for people who do not have symptoms.

27TH OCTOBER

It's been three days since my test, and still nothing. Between the first test coming back inconclusive and hanging on for so long for the results of this one, this has got to be the longest test wait ever. I check my phone at least once an hour. It's relentless. My pregnancy test came back quicker than this. Perhaps if I had peed on the swab, the results would have come back quicker! I phoned the test centre in case my results had been lost. The man on the phone said I had to wait five days before he could do anything. So, yep, you guessed it, more waiting.

In the UK, a further 22,885 coronavirus cases have been recorded, along with 367 deaths.

28TH OCTOBER

At 3 pm yesterday, I finally got my result... negative! Dave's was negative, too. A massive weight has been lifted and my freedom returned. I was over the moon, even though it had been a long time coming. Last night, I slept really well.

In Scotland, 28 people have died from Covid-19 in the past 24 hours.

Wales has recorded its highest number of deaths since April.

In the UK, 24,701 new coronavirus cases have been recorded, along with 310 deaths.

Germany is embarking on a four-week lockdown. Meanwhile, a second national lockdown is set to begin in France within days.

30TH OCTOBER

It's Halloween tomorrow, but I haven't put any decorations up as there won't be any trick or treaters, so what's the point? We'll just watch a Halloween-themed family film instead. Hopefully, next year will be better. In the meantime, we'll focus on making Christmas as good as possible instead.

In the UK, 23,065 new coronavirus cases have been reported, along with 280 deaths.

ONS (Office for National Statistics) figures suggest that just last week, more than 560,000 people had coronavirus in England.

31ST OCTOBER

The total number of confirmed coronavirus cases in the UK has surpassed one million.

A further 21,915 cases were confirmed, along with 326 deaths.

As I write, I am waiting for the PM to address the nation. Rumours have been circulating online about a month-long nationwide lockdown.

An hour later… I have just finished watching Boris Johnson shut down the country again. People in England will only be allowed to leave their homes for specific reasons, such as education, work or food shopping. Schools, colleges and universities will remain open. Those who can will be expected to work from home.

Pubs, bars and restaurants will close across the country, although they will be able to offer takeaway and delivery services.

Non-essential shops, hairdressers, and leisure and entertainment venues will also be shut, as will gyms.

Different households will be banned from mixing.

People will be able to travel for work but will not be allowed to go abroad for holidays.

Angel was meant to depart for Costa Rica on 7th November. To avoid the lockdown restrictions, she has now decided to bring her trip forward to 4th November. Costa Rica has recorded 109,971 cases and 1,385 deaths.

Here's an update on what's happening in some other countries around the world.

- The USA has recorded 9,404,764 cases and 236,098 deaths.
- India has recorded 8,185,881 cases and 122,160 deaths.
- Brazil has recorded 5,535,605 cases and 159,902 deaths.
- Russia has recorded 1,636,781 cases and 28,235 deaths.
- The UK has recorded 1,011,660 cases and 46,555 deaths.

My theory is that we need a way of testing the super-spreaders. Right now, you can only get a test if you have symptoms or have been told to by Track and Trace. If we could pinpoint the people who unwittingly have it by testing them, we could prevent the spread. In other words, we need mass testing.

I also read somewhere that UV light kills Covid, so why doesn't the government bulk-buy UV lights for the public to keep in their houses for the duration of the four-week lockdown? That way, we'd be killing the virus without doing anything out of the ordinary. It seems like a potential solution to me.

2ND NOVEMBER

In the latest 24-hour period, the UK has recorded a further 18,950 coronavirus cases, along with 136 deaths, bringing the total death toll to 46,853.

10,918 patients are currently in hospital battling the virus, 978 of whom are on ventilators.

Australia has reported zero Covid cases for first time in five months.

As a result of the new lockdown, all my cat-sitting clients have cancelled for this month. It's disappointing though hardly surprising.

3RD NOVEMBER

A further 397 people have died after testing positive for coronavirus. It's the highest daily number since May.

4TH NOVEMBER

Tragically, a further 492 people have lost their lives to this dreadful virus. From midnight tonight, NHS England is to move to the highest alert level. They are warning of a serious situation ahead.

5TH NOVEMBER

LOCKDOWN 2.0

Angel left for Costa Rica yesterday. She has gone for six months. I'm praying she stays safe. Her holiday destination has recorded 113,261 cases so far and 1,431 deaths.

As of today, and until 2nd December, I can only leave home for the essentials. There are a few exceptions this time round, as follows:

- People can leave their home to attend an event commemorating Remembrance Sunday. They can also visit estate agencies and show homes and move house. Visits to waste disposal or recycling centres are also allowed.
- There is to be no mixing between different households inside or outside the home unless that other household is part of your support bubble.
- Overnight stays and holidays away from your home are not permitted, including holidays in the UK and abroad. The ban includes stays in second homes.
- Children are allowed to move between different homes if their parents are separated.
- Outdoor exercise and recreation is encouraged and is unlimited, but only with your household bubble, on your own or with one other person from a different household. Golf is not allowed.
- Wedding and civil partnership ceremonies will not be allowed except in exceptional circumstances.
- Services in places of worship are banned, but private prayer is permitted.
- Funerals are allowed to continue with a maximum of 30 people, with only close friends and family advised to attend.

Angel texted me today saying she has safely reached Costa Rica. I am really going to miss her. I hope she has an amazing time.

6TH NOVEMBER

The UK has recorded a further 23,287 coronavirus cases, and a further 355 people have died.
The UK R number remains at 1.1 to 1.3.

7TH NOVEMBER

It feels like the virus is closing in again. I have heard of two people in our village coming down with it, as well as a close relative of one of the residents. At this point, I can't see how anyone is going to escape it; the numbers are too high. I think it will hit us all eventually, and I also think a month's lockdown won't be sufficient to bring cases down.

Greece has entered its second lockdown, which is set to last for three weeks. Every time someone wants to go out, they will be required to send a text message to a five-digit number providing their name, address and their reason for leaving the house. The country recorded 2,917 new infections recently, its highest daily tally since the outbreak began in February. While the death rate is still comparatively low compared to other countries, it is on the rise.

Here's an update on the situation in some other countries around the world.

- The USA has recorded 10,071,095 cases and 242,339 deaths.
- India has recorded 8,478,689 cases and 125,895 deaths.
- Brazil has recorded 5,632,505 cases and 162,035 deaths.
- Russia has recorded 1,753,836 cases and 30,251 deaths.

- France has recorded 1,661,853 cases and 39,865 deaths.
- Spain has recorded 1,388,411 cases and 38,833 deaths.
- Argentina has recorded 1,228,814 cases and 33,136 deaths.
- The UK has recorded 1,146,484 cases and 48,475 deaths.
- Costa Rica has recorded 115,417 cases and 1,453 deaths.

It's scary how Covid-19 has spread throughout the whole world, with many countries locking down for the second time. My heart goes out to all those families who have lost someone to the virus. What a truly awful year it has been.

8TH NOVEMBER

The UK has recorded a further 20,572 coronavirus cases, and an additional 156 people have lost their life.

9TH NOVEMBER

I was awake in bed at 1 am this morning thinking of the high number of coronavirus cases in the UK. A few things popped into my head, as follows. Are masks actually working? Also, a few months ago, a house cat was found to have coronavirus, which it caught from its owners. With such a high number of current cases, why aren't more house pets coming down with the virus? I also have a wild theory about rats picking the virus up in our drains and then spreading it about. I have no idea of the science behind this. As I said, it's just a wild theory.

Perhaps it's time to return to the real facts…

Since the beginning of the pandemic, there have been more than 50 million positive cases worldwide. Almost 10 million of these were in the USA, even though the country is host to only around four percent of the world's population. Recently, the USA reported more than 126,000 positive cases and more than 1,000 deaths of people with the virus in a 24-hour period.

Data has shown that October was the worst month for the pandemic so far.

India has recorded some 8.5 million cases, while the UK accounts for almost 1.2 million of the world's total cases. Across the globe, 1.2 million people have died from the virus.

The firebreak lockdown in Wales ends today, and new national measures to combat the virus have come into effect.

Now for some good news. A vaccine has been announced! In a great day for science and humanity, the Pfizer/BioNTech Covid-19 vaccine has been found to be 90 percent effective in preventing people from getting the virus.

Phase three of the vaccine trial involved 43,538 participants from six countries. They received two doses of either the immunisation or a placebo, with 90 percent of the people who took the vaccines protected from the virus within 28 days of having their injections. Only 94 people who took part in the trial went on to develop coronavirus, and no serious safety concerns were reported.

The minks have come up again, this time in Denmark, where several are infected with the virus. The WHO says the minks contracted Covid-19 following exposure to infected humans. Apparently, the animals can act as a 'reservoir', passing the virus between them and to humans. The Danish government has ordered the cull of 15 million minks from more than a thousand farms. It has also imposed lockdown restrictions on more than a quarter of a million Danes in a northern region of the country.

Due to concerns about the outbreak on mink farms, all non-British national or resident travellers who have been to Denmark in the past fortnight have been denied entry to the country.

Boris Johnson said tonight that although the coronavirus vaccine has cleared a significant hurdle, there are more to overcome before it can be widely rolled out.

In September, a draft list was published showing who was likely to be at the front of the queue for a jab once a coronavirus vaccine is approved in the UK.

This is the priority list:

1. Older adults, residents in care homes and care home workers.
2. All those 80 years of age and over and health and social care workers.
3. All those 75 years of age and over.
4. All those 70 years of age and over.
5. All those 65 years of age and over.
6. High-risk adults under 65 years of age.
7. Moderate-risk adults under 65 years of age.
8. All those 60 years of age and over.
9. All those 55 years of age and over.
10. All those 50 years of age and over.
11. Rest of the population (priority to be determined).
12. ME!!!!!!!!!!!!!!!!

According to WHO, globally almost 40 potential vaccines are being tested, and more than 140 others are in the early stages of testing. However, experts have said that just one in 10 of the world's population is likely to be protected against Covid-19 in the first year of a vaccine being made available.

Analysis of global manufacturing capacity shows that even if a vaccine is given the green light, just two billion doses could be produced in 2021.

A further 194 people with coronavirus have died across the UK in the latest 24-hour period. This brings the total death toll to 49,238. However, separate figures published by the UK's statistics agencies for deaths where Covid-19 was mentioned on the death certificate, together with additional data, show there have now been 65,000 deaths involving coronavirus in the UK.

The number of confirmed cases across the country has now reached 1,213 million.

10ᵀᴴ NOVEMBER

The Secretary of State has asked the NHS to be ready to deploy the Covid-19 vaccine from the start of December.

Lockdown has been named as the *Collins Dictionary* Word of the Year. With many countries entering a second lockdown, it is not a word to celebrate, but it is one that sums up the year for many people around the world.

The number of confirmed coronavirus cases in the USA has surpassed 10 million.

My daughter has been back at school for a while now, and luckily there have been no Covid scares so far. It's such a relief, and it's nice for her to have her lessons back and be able to socialise with her classmates again.

This lockdown feels different to the last one. Many more shops are open, and more people are out and about. My daughter asked today if Christmas is cancelled because of coronavirus, and can we still put the decorations up? I told her that it might feel a little different this year, but it would still be special, and we'd have the decorations up as usual.

People with suspected coronavirus in Naples, Italy, have been given oxygen in their cars after the hospital was overwhelmed with patients. A local resident said he was worried after being unable to get information about his father's condition. He said he called a doctor, who'd told him all the medics on the ward were in isolation because they had the virus.

Meanwhile, closer to home, mass testing for coronavirus is being trialled in Liverpool, including for people who aren't displaying symptoms. Lateral flow tests, which use similar technology to pregnancy tests and have a turnaround time of under an hour, have been available since Friday for the people who live and work in the city.

The UK has recorded a further 532 Covid-related deaths, bringing the death toll to 49,770. A further 20,412 people have tested positive for the virus.

11TH NOVEMBER

According to a new study, almost seven out of 10 patients hospitalised due to coronavirus still suffer from debilitating symptoms more than seven weeks after being discharged. The research team found that 54 days after discharge, 69 percent of patients were experiencing fatigue and 53 percent were suffering from persistent breathlessness. They also found that 34 percent still had a cough and 15 percent reported depression. In addition, 38 percent of chest radiographs remained abnormal, and nine percent were getting worse.

In Nepal, Covid cases have surpassed, 200,000 amid fears of a health catastrophe.

Switzerland has recorded 8,270 new coronavirus cases.

I spoke to a friend who recently came down with the virus. She said she lost her sense of smell first, and then the muscles in her legs started to ache and she felt incredibly tired. She also had a dodgy tummy and constantly went from hot to cold, although her feet remained like ice. Luckily, she is now feeling a lot better and thinks she is over the worst of it.

12TH NOVEMBER

Last night, I came down with a sore throat and felt achy. I went to bed at 9.30 pm and woke up this morning feeling better. I still have a slight sore throat, but my paranoia over having Covid has eased a bit. Dave had an op booked in before the first lockdown, but it was put on hold because of the pandemic. He has finally been given his new date – 8th January.

There have been some tragic stories in the news about recent Covid victims. These have included the oldest known victim – a 108-year-old who had survived the Spanish flu pandemic – and the youngest, a 13-day-old baby.

The UK has recorded a further 33,470 daily cases compared to 22,950 yesterday. This is the highest daily number recorded since the outbreak. A further 595 people have died, bringing the total death toll to over 50,000.

13TH NOVEMBER

So, today is the dreaded Friday the 13th, if you believe in that sort of thing.

I've been thinking about how Covid is transmitted. I've heard of a couple of people who have come down with the virus without passing it on to the rest of their household. How this can happen is a mystery to me, because presumably they were in close contact with them on a regular basis.

France's R number has fallen below 1, but the number of people in hospital has hit a new high, with someone being admitted every 30 seconds.

The UK has recorded a further 27,301 positive cases, along with 376 deaths. The total number of confirmed cases since the pandemic began is now 1,317,496.

16TH NOVEMBER

I thought I'd get into the festivities early and put my Christmas decorations up. I know that's a bit daft, but it has been a rubbish year so far. I haven't gone as far as getting the tree, but the house in general is looking twinklier.

The UK has secured five million doses of the Moderna vaccine, which is said to be almost 95 percent effective.

18TH NOVEMBER

The deaths of a further 598 people with coronavirus were announced yesterday – the highest daily figure since early May. Another 20,051 cases have also been recorded.

Boris Johnson has tested negative for the virus after recently coming into contact with an infected person.

Meanwhile, a member of staff at my daughter's school has tested positive, and two other staff members are self-isolating after coming into contact with them. I have chosen to take my daughter out of school for two weeks in case of a wider outbreak.

21ST NOVEMBER

The NHS is hoping to begin vaccinating people against coronavirus from as early as next month.

The UK has recorded a further 19,875 cases, along with 341 deaths.

22ND NOVEMBER

Today, my daughter and I made gingerbread people, stars, unicorns and dinosaurs. I love the way baking gingerbread makes the house smell like Christmas.

The UK has recorded a further 18,662 cases and 398 deaths.

23RD NOVEMBER

Boris Johnson has said that when national restrictions end on 2nd December, we will return to a regional, tiered approach to fighting the virus.

The UK has recorded a further 15,450 cases and 206 deaths.

25TH NOVEMBER

Today, we made some gingerbread cats – a bit predictable for our house! They looked and tasted delicious.

The UK has recorded 696 Covid-related deaths. Yesterday's figure was 608.

27TH NOVEMBER

At last, some positive news. The UK's R number has fallen to between 0.9 and 1.

28TH NOVEMBER

We bought and decorated our Christmas tree today. I can't wait until the festive season truly arrives, as then we can hide from Covid under blankets while watching Xmas movies, drinking hot chocolate and eating gingerbread.

The UK has recorded a further 15,871 coronavirus cases and 479 deaths.

Schools have been sending year groups home because of children testing positive.

30TH NOVEMBER

I spoke to Angel today; she is having a great time in Costa Rica and says it's really hot. Lucky girl.

1ST DECEMBER

My daughter goes back to school tomorrow, and then there's only a few weeks until Christmas. We'll make the most of it, as we've been told we'll all have to self-isolate before Dave's op in January. The month-long lockdown ends tomorrow, so businesses can get up and running again.

Here's an update on the Covid situation around the world.

- The USA has recorded 13,920,038 cases and 274,332 deaths.
- India has recorded 9,463,254 cases and 137,659 deaths.
- Brazil has recorded 6,336,278 cases and 173,165 deaths.
- Russia has recorded 2,322,056 cases and 40,464 deaths.

- France has recorded 2,322,056 cases and 52,731 deaths.
- Spain has recorded 1,664,945 cases and 45,069 deaths.
- The UK has recorded 1,629,657 cases and 58,448 deaths.
- Italy has recorded 1,601,554 cases and 55,576 deaths.

As of tomorrow, we will return to a tier system. Here's an outline of the three tiers and what they will involve:

Tier 1: medium alert

Rule of six applies indoors and outdoors. Hospitality venues can remain open with table service and an 11 pm curfew. Limited spectators at sport and live entertainment.

Tier 2: high alert

No household mixing indoors, with the rule of six applied outdoors. Pubs and bars should remain closed unless operating as restaurants. Journey numbers should be reduced where possible.

Tier 3: very high alert

No household mixing in most settings, takeaway only for all hospitality venues, travel outside the area should be avoided.

My area is currently in tier 2.

· · ·

The UK has recorded 13,430 new coronavirus cases, along with 603 deaths.

3ʳᵈ DECEMBER

The UK has become the first country in the world to approve the Pfizer/BioNTech Covid-19 vaccine for use. The government has secured 40 million doses of the vaccine and patients will require two doses. This means there aren't enough shots to vaccinate the entire population, though the roll-out will begin from next week.

The USA has recorded its biggest daily death toll of the pandemic so far, on the same day as a record number of Covid-19 patients were in hospital. A tragic 2,670 coronavirus deaths were recorded – the equivalent of nearly two deaths a minute.

Here in the UK, a total of more than 60,000 people have now died after contracting the virus.

6ᵀᴴ DECEMBER

We bought our turkey today, and all our festive nibbles. I have been constantly playing Christmas music in my car, and I've already bought and wrapped all the presents. Go me!!!

We need something to make us feel warm and fuzzy inside; this year has been so different, and not in a nice way.

On Friday, the UK's R number was estimated to be between 0.8 and 1.0, suggesting a slight fall compared with the previous week.

7TH DECEMBER

The UK has recorded a further 14,718 coronavirus cases and 189 deaths.

8TH DECEMBER

It's been a historic day, as a 90-year-old woman has become the first person to receive the Pfizer/BioNTech vaccine as part of a vaccination programme. She was given the jab in a hospital at 6.31 am this morning and, since she turns 91 next week, she said getting the jab was the best early birthday present she could wish for, as it means she can spend time with her family and friends after being on her own for most of the year.

Last week, the UK became the first country in the world to approve the vaccine.

Vaccinations will be given at dozens of hospital hubs from today. People aged 80 and over, and care home workers, will be among the first to receive the jab, which needs to be refrigerated at -70C (-94F).

9TH DECEMBER

UK regulators have warned people with a history of significant allergic reactions not to have the Pfizer/BioNTech jab. This comes after two NHS staff members fell ill after being vaccinated. They are now understood to be recovering.

10TH DECEMBER

London has the highest coronavirus case rates in England, but nationwide, infection rates have plateaued.

12TH DECEMBER

The USA has approved the Pfizer/BioNT vaccine, with the first jab set to be administered in less than 24 hours. This marks a turning point in America, where the pandemic has killed more than 295,000 people.

13TH DECEMBER

One more week of school and that's it, I'm ready for Christmas. Dave has finished work, so I'm looking forward to doing nothing except watching Christmas movies, singing Christmas songs, eating Christmas goodies, making more gingerbread and being with my family.

The UK has recorded a further 18,4447 coronavirus cases and 144 deaths.

14TH DECEMBER

A new variant of coronavirus has been identified in the UK. It is believed to be causing the faster spread of the virus in the South East. London will move into tier 3.

15TH DECEMBER

The UK has recorded a further 18,450 coronavirus cases and 506 deaths. It's been said that vaccinating the entire UK population could take up to a year, even with no interruptions. In living memory, no country has mounted a whole-population vaccination campaign.

A 104-year-old in Spain has been applauded by nurses after recovering from coronavirus.

Some countries are putting restrictions in place for the

Christmas period. Here's a rundown of what some are doing:

The Netherlands A second lockdown is set to start soon, lasting for at least five weeks. Dutch households will be banned from having more than two visitors over the age of 13, and all public places, including hairdressers and day care centres, will close until 19th January. Schools will close until 18th January, and people have been advised to stay at home, not travel to work and avoid contact with others as much as possible. From 24th until 26th December, households will be allowed three visitors.

Czech Republic Restaurants, hotels and indoor sports venues, which reopened barely two weeks ago, will close again from the end of the week. Public gatherings will be limited to six people indoors and out, and a nationwide curfew will run from 11 am to 5 am. Schools will close early for Christmas, although shops will remain open.

Germany A hard lockdown in Germany begins soon, with schools and non-essential shops to be closed throughout the Christmas and New Year period. Germany has been under a light lockdown since the beginning of November, with bars, restaurants and tourist attractions closed, but shopping and education allowed. The new restrictions will last until 10th January but will be relaxed slightly from 24th to 26th December, with a five-person limit on mixing. Drinking will be banned in public, and in the run-up to New Year's Eve, firework sales will be prohibited. Religious gatherings will be allowed but only if people remain 1.5 metres apart and refrain from singing.

France A six-week ban on movement was lifted on Tuesday, but the President imposed an 8 pm to 6 am curfew until mid-January, with the exception of Christmas Eve. Museums, theatres and cinemas will be closed until January at least, as will restaurants, bars and cafés. A maximum of six adults and any number of children are allowed to mix indoors. French ski resorts will remain closed and only be allowed to reopen again in January "under favourable conditions".

Spain From 23rd December to 6th January, travel between Spain's regions will be allowed, but only to visit friends and family. Social gatherings on Christmas Eve, Christmas Day, New Year's Eve and New Year's Day will be limited to 10 people – including children.

Curfews, which currently range from 10 pm to midnight, depending on the region, will be pushed back to 1.30 am on Christmas Eve and New Year's Eve.

Italy A ban on travelling between different regions will be in place from 21st December to 6th January, and people will be banned from leaving their hometowns on Christmas Day, Boxing Day and New Year's Day.

The current 10 pm to 5 am curfew will remain, meaning traditional Midnight Mass won't happen, although churches can remain open. The Italian Prime Minister told citizens to expect a "more sober Christmas without Christmas Eve gatherings, hugs and kisses".

Rome is expected to impose a 'red zone' lockdown from Christmas Eve until at least 2nd January, with night curfews extended, bans on non-essential movement and non-essential shops to close.

All these restrictions are being put into place because Italy is experiencing its highest number of deaths since the end of March. The total death toll now stands at 65,000.

Austria Restrictions have been eased ahead of Christmas, after the country came out of its second national lockdown on 7th December. A curfew has been introduced between 8 pm and 6 am, and non-essential shops and other businesses have re-opened. Restaurants and bars will remain closed over the Christmas period for everything but takeaways.

Hotels are only open to business travellers, and people visiting from countries with more than 100 cases per 100,000 people will be required to quarantine for 10 days.

Portugal Rules will be eased over the Christmas season to allow people to visit their friends and family, but measures will be re-imposed ahead of New Year's Eve. A 10-person gathering limit will be lifted entirely for Christmas, and the curfew will be pushed from 11 pm to 2 am on 24th and 25th December.

Here in the UK, plans are afoot to allow up to three households to form a Christmas bubble and meet for five days between 23rd and 27th December. Travel restrictions will also be lifted during the same five-day period.

I've also been reading about how the virus is developing and mutating over time. It's pretty interesting. So far, there have been at least seven major groups or strains of Covid-19, as it adapts to its human hosts. The original strain, discovered in the Chinese city of Wuhan in December last year, is known as the L strain, which then mutated into the S strain at the beginning of 2020, before being followed by the V and G strains. Strain G has been mostly found in Europe and North America, but because these continents were slow to restrict movement, it allowed the virus to spread faster and therefore mutate further into strains GR, GH and GV. Meanwhile, the original L strain persisted for longer in Asia because several countries, including China, were quick to shut their borders and stop movement. Several other, less frequent mutations are grouped together as strain O.

G strains are now dominant around the world, particularly in Italy and Europe, and this has coincided with spikes in outbreaks. A specific mutation – D614G – is the most common variant. Some experts say this variation has made the virus more infectious, but other studies have contradicted this. Meanwhile, earlier strains, such as the original L strain and the V strain, are gradually disappearing.

16TH DECEMBER

Over the past seven days, the number of Covid vaccines administered in the UK were as follows:

- 108,000 in England
- 7,897 in Wales
- 18,000 in Scotland

Meanwhile, the UK has recorded 25,161 new cases and 612 deaths.

17TH DECEMBER

From the weekend, my area is to move into tier 3.

The French President, Emmanuel Macron, has tested positive for the virus.

Northern Ireland is to enter a six-week lockdown from Boxing Day.

The UK has recorded a further 35,383 coronavirus cases and 532 deaths.

18TH DECEMBER

The UK's R number has risen to between 1.1 and 1.2. Last week, it was between 0.9 and 1.

School finished today, and we are all still Covid free, so Christmas has officially begun.

The UK has recorded a further 28,507 cases and 489 deaths.

We are now officially in tier 3, but it has already been announced that from tomorrow, we will move into a new tier. Millions of people across England are in the same boat. Being in tier 4 means they will no longer be able to mix with other households at Christmas. Boris Johnson explained tonight that the drastic move has been prompted by fears over a new strain of coronavirus. He also announced the planned five-day easing of restrictions over the festive period will now be limited to a single day for everyone who isn't in tier 4. They will still be able to mix in private homes with up to two other households, but only on 25ᵗʰ December. The tier 4 measures will see all non-essential shops, gyms and hairdressers close, with people ordered to stay home, apart from limited exceptions such as work. The new strain is believed to spread more quickly than the original one, although there's no evidence that it causes more severe illness or higher mortality. This strain has also been detected in two other countries other than the UK, albeit in very small quantities.

Personally, I'm glad we are having a Christmas lockdown. If people visit their families, they may have a good time, but they might not all make it into the new year. What's missing one Christmas if it means you get to celebrate the next one? It doesn't affect us too much, as it's always just the three of us, but if we did have the option of visiting other households, I'd want to stay away until it was safe.

In other news, more than 60 clinics have been opened in England to help the thousands of people suffering from long-term symptoms of coronavirus. According to the ONS, around 186,000 people have suffered symptoms for up to 12 weeks.

A further 28,507 cases have been recorded, along with 489 deaths.

20ᵀᴴ DECEMBER

A further 35,928 coronavirus cases have been recorded across the UK, along with 326 deaths.

21ˢᵀ DECEMBER

The new coronavirus strain that is spreading rapidly in the UK has also been detected in Denmark, Gibraltar and the Netherlands. France and South Africa also believe they have cases of the mutation, but these are yet to be confirmed.

The strain, which was first detected in London and the South East earlier this month, is up to 70 percent more infectious than the original one. This is because it has a much bigger viral load. It is now present in all parts of the UK, with the exception of Northern Ireland.

In the UK, a further 33,364 new coronavirus cases have been recorded, along with 215 deaths.

22ᴺᴰ DECEMBER

The UK has recorded its highest daily increase in Covid-19 cases, with 36,804 new infections and 691 deaths.

I spoke to Angel today, and she seems happy in sunny Costa Rica, although she did say she had a snake in her room last night, which I thought was hilarious. She said she managed to remove it by pushing it out with a broom. She also told me how she was lying in bed when she heard a tapping at the window. She got up, opened the curtains and saw that it was a racoon. She sent me a photo of the animal, and it was adorable. I said she should have let it in and had a cuddle with it. She said I was mad to suggest that!

28TH DECEMBER

So that was it, we did Christmas, and we had a great time. We sang songs, watched movies, ate chocolate and opened presents. It was just what we all needed.

The weather forecast predicted snow today. My daughter was so excited, but in the end, it didn't arrive, so instead of sledging we put the Christmas decorations away.

People suffering from long Covid are reporting smelling fish, sulphur and a sweet, sickly odour, as further symptoms of the virus emerge. The unusual side effect is known as parosmia, meaning a distortion of smell.

A further 41,385 new Covid cases have been recorded in the UK; it's the highest daily increase since the pandemic began. There have also been a further 357 deaths. The overall death toll now stands at 71,109.

29TH DECEMBER

The first patient to receive the Pfizer/BioNTech vaccine got their second jab today.

Meanwhile, the rest of the news made for scary reading. A further 53,135 new infections have been recorded in the last 24 hours, and 414 deaths.

I now know five people who have survived Covid, so I'm guessing they are walking around feeling pretty invincible. It seems rare for people to get it twice. So, technically, they have their normal lives back while the rest of us still feel like we're dodging bullets.

I spoke to Angel again tonight, and she had a nice Christmas in Costa Rica.

30TH DECEMBER

Dave's operation was cancelled because the hospital staff need to concentrate on caring for Covid patients. It's understandable, but also frustrating, as he has been waiting for a year now. Hopefully, he won't have to wait too much longer.

The Oxford-AstraZeneca Covid-19 vaccine has become the second jab approved for UK roll-out. It provides 70 percent effectiveness against the virus 22 days after the first dose.

The UK has recorded 50,023 new Covid cases and 981 deaths. Today's death toll is the highest since 24th April.

I'm so scared by the number of cases and deaths. They seem to have rapidly increased, and I'd been hoping the Christmas period would help bring the numbers down.

From tomorrow, more areas are moving into tier 4. In total, 44 million people (78 percent of England's population) will be living under the harshest restrictions.

A further 12 million people will be in tier 3, with no areas being deemed safe enough for tier 2.

It's clear that this new, highly transmissible variant is spreading through England like wildfire, and cases are doubling fast.

Ireland has returned to a full lockdown for at least a month.

31ST DECEMBER

It's New Year's Eve, and the whole of the UK will be staying home. We'll be having party food for dinner, and then we'll watch a movie and play a board game. We might even do a little dance to see in the new year, which we can only hope will be better than this one.

Meanwhile, Nightingale Hospitals across England are being readied for use. This comes as the UK records a new daily high of 55,892 coronavirus cases. There have also been a further 964 deaths.

The new variant has now been detected in China and Southern California.

What this year has taught me is how necessary human contact is, be it mental or physical. We are creatures of habit who enjoy being around each other.

As 2020 draws to a close, I've brought together the total cases and total deaths in countries around the world.

USA
Total cases: 20,237,964
Total deaths: 351,127
India
Total cases: 10,282,624
Total deaths: 148,950
Brazil
Total cases: 7,619,970
Total deaths: 193,940
Russia
Total cases: 3,159,297
Total deaths: 57,019
France
Total cases: 2,600,498
Total deaths: 64,381
UK
Total cases: 2,488,780
Total deaths: 73,512
Turkey
Total cases: 2,208,652
Total deaths: 20,881
Italy

Total cases: 2,107,166
Total deaths: 74,159
Spain
Total cases: 1,921,155
Total deaths: 50,689
Germany
Total cases: 1,735,819
Total deaths: 33,917
Columbia
Total cases: 1,626,461
Total deaths: 42,909
Argentina
Total cases: 1,613,928
Total deaths: 43,163
Mexico
Total cases: 1,413,935
Total deaths: 124,897
Poland
Total cases: 1,294,878
Total deaths: 28,554
Costa Rica
Total cases: 168,114
Total deaths: 2,171

COVID 2021

1ST JANUARY, 2021

Happy New Year!
We watched the countdown to 2021 on TV, and unexpectedly, there were fireworks. It was a lovely surprise as it would have been awful without them. So, here's to a new year; let's hope we can get rid of Covid for good.

The UK has recorded 53,285 new cases and 613 deaths. So far, a million Brits have received a Covid vaccine.

2ND JANUARY

The UK has recorded 57,725 new cases, its highest daily total since the start of the pandemic. A further 445 people have sadly lost their life.

3ʳᴰ JANUARY

The UK has recorded more than 50,000 new Covid cases for the sixth day running, and there have been a further 454 deaths. The total death toll has now surpassed 75,000.

4ᵀᴴ JANUARY

Scotland has announced a national lockdown starting from midnight.

So, that's Scotland in lockdown and Ireland in lockdown… With cases rising in England, what exactly are we waiting for? My daughter goes back to school on Wednesday, but I don't feel comfortable sending her there while cases are this high. If the new strain is causing this crazy spread, why would I put her in the firing line? So, tonight I have decided not to send her back to school for two weeks. The numbers are too high and it's too much of a risk.

The UK has recorded 58,784 new coronavirus cases and 407 deaths. In total, 2,713,563 people have tested positive for the virus.

Update. In an address to the nation at 8 pm, the PM announced a new national lockdown for England. We are now being asked to stay at home like we did back in March. If cases drop enough, schools may reopen in mid-February. So, this is our third national lockdown.

5ᵀᴴ JANUARY

Lockdown 3.0 (also known as third time lucky).

Last night, Dave went out just after the lockdown was announced to get some shopping in. He was worried about people flocking to the shops en masse today and clearing the shelves. When he came home, I washed all the shopping, just like I did in the old days of Lockdown 1.0.

A further 60,916 people have tested positive in the UK, and there have been 830 deaths. It's getting even scarier.

The PM has said that more than a million people in England are currently infected with coronavirus.

6TH JANUARY

It's Day One of home schooling. After enjoying some Christmas lie-ins, it was hard getting out of bed early, but we managed it. My daughter went on Zoom and then we did some online learning, then more Zoom. All in all, it was a good day.

When my daughter was in baby group, we used to sing to her: *Zoom, zoom, zoom, we are going to the moon*. Do you think this was to prepare her for the Zoom calls she's having now?

The clapping is back! It's been renamed Clap for Heroes, and it starts on Thursday at 8 pm. It's to pay tribute to everyone who has played their part during the pandemic. I'm happy that we can once again show our appreciation for these amazing people who have worked so tirelessly.

The UK has recorded a further 63,322 new cases and 1,041 deaths. This is the highest number of deaths in 24 hours since 21st April 2020. Also, this is the tenth time since the pandemic began that the daily number of deaths has exceeded 1,000. The number of Covid patients in the UK has also passed 30,000 for the first time. Across the UK, 2,645 hospital patients are on ventilators.

The government has revealed the locations of seven mass vaccination centres. They are in Stevenage, London, Newcastle, Manchester, Surrey, Bristol and Birmingham.

So far, a total of 1.3 million doses of the Covid vaccine have been administered throughout the UK.

7TH JANUARY

Another successful day of home schooling. My daughter seems to be enjoying it, which is good, though I'm starting to miss seeing people. I miss hugging my friends, and I miss laughing with them and sharing creative ideas. I would like to think and talk about anything other than Covid. I also miss sunshine, which makes everything more bearable. It was -1 degrees today, and cold and gloomy. I miss Angel and our spontaneous cups of tea and chats about nonsense.

The UK has recorded a further 52,618 cases and 1,162 deaths.

At 8 pm, I duly went out and clapped. Hardly anyone else was out, and it was cold and dark. It didn't feel like everyone was united this time. Very disappointing.

8TH JANUARY

The Moderna vaccine has become the third Covid jab approved for use in the UK, with an additional 10 million doses ordered. The vaccine, which is produced by a company in the US, was shown to have 94 percent efficacy.

UK Covid-19 vaccines:

Oxford-AstraZeneca
Doses ordered: 100 million
Cost per dose: £3
Storage: Fridge
Pfizer/BioNTech
Doses ordered: 40 million
Cost per does: £15
Storage: -70 C

Moderna
Doses ordered: 7 million
Cost per dose: £28
Storage: -20 C

The Mayor of London, Sadiq Khan, has declared a "major incident" in the capital due to rising coronavirus cases, which are threatening to overwhelm hospitals. More than 800 patients a day are being admitted to London hospitals with the virus.

As part of her home schooling, my daughter had to do a collage of a fruit bowl. We had loads of fun making it, using a banana skin for the banana, a Quality Street wrapper for the orange, ripped-up green paper for the grapes and a red piece of paper torn from a magazine for the apple. We even collected twigs from outside to represent the grape stems and apple stalks.

The UK has recorded 68,053 new coronavirus cases and 1,325 deaths.

9TH JANUARY

The Queen and the Duke of Edinburgh are to receive their first dose of the vaccine.

A further 59,937 new cases have been recorded in the UK, and 1,035 deaths. The total death toll has now surpassed 80,000.

Approximately 1.5 million vaccines have been administered so far.

10TH JANUARY

The UK has recorded 54,940 new cases and 563 deaths.

Since the pandemic began, there have been more than

three million confirmed cases here – the fifth highest in the world.

Still, more than 200,000 people are receiving their vaccine every day, and the government is on course to reach its target of two million vaccinations a week. However, the current pressure on the NHS is bad. The ambulance service is also facing unprecedented call-outs. It's been reported that ambulances are waiting up to nine hours to offload patients at London hospitals, and many people with non-life-threatening emergencies are having to wait up to 10 hours for an ambulance. The Metropolitan Police announced that it will deploy 75 officers to drive ambulances in the capital.

I spoke to Angel tonight, and she said it was raining in Costa Rica. I asked her what she'd been up to, and she had been horse riding and zip wiring through the jungle, though she got stuck, which I found hilarious. Some locals cooked her a giant fish in a huge pot, and she gets woken up by birds every morning. She also has a bat in her bedroom that only comes out at night. Then she asked what I had been up to. *Hmmm.* I told her we were in lockdown again and that I had bought some really nice new pyjamas online and made a Lego house with my daughter. I also reported that she had a wobbly tooth. Wow, lockdown life really does sound boring!

11ᵗʰ JANUARY

I've been having a text conversation with my fit and healthy friend, who, like me, is right at the bottom of the vaccine list.

> Me: So, I was just thinking, if the vaccine mutates everyone and turns them into something else, the only people that will be left to deal with the end of the world will be me, you and Angel. So, what shall we do at the end of the world? Wanna learn how to fly a plane? Climb Big Ben? Jog around Buckingham Palace? Sleep in Windsor Castle?

> Friend: Oh, let's check out Buckingham Palace. Can we raid a chocolate factory? It wouldn't matter if we got really fat. Just had a thought. We would be left with all the kids in the world, as they won't have had the vaccine either. Maybe I will become Queen.

> Me: Raid a chocolate factory... that means I will have to hold your hair back while you throw up, thanks for that. I'll let you be Queen if I can be Queen of all the world's cats.

> Friend: I will never be sick from chocolate; it's a stable dietary requirement – like fruit and veg. Ha ha.

In between our conversation, I texted Angel and explained the gist of our chat.

> Angel: Can I be Queen of the chocolate factory?

So, it's officially the end of the world, and out of the three remaining survivors, two of them are talking about chocolate!!!

In England, 374,613 people have received a second dose of the Covid vaccine.

In the UK, 46,169 new cases have been recorded, along

with 529 deaths. Of the 32,070 Covid patients in UK hospitals, 3,055 are in mechanical ventilation beds.

12TH JANUARY

In 2020, the number of excess deaths, as a proportion of the population, rose by 12.1 percent in the UK compared with the average of the previous five years. To put that into perspective, that's the biggest leap in any year since 1940. This shows how, even though the pandemic is ongoing, it has already exerted an extraordinary cost in terms of lives lost. This has happened despite some of the most severe lockdown restrictions ever endured. The toll of Covid-19 is becoming clearer, and the statistics are thoroughly depressing.

Israel has vaccinated more than 15 percent of its population and the USA has vaccinated more than one percent. The UK is somewhere in between, though the government has promised to vaccinate nearly 14 million by the middle of February 2021.

Today, a further 45,533 new coronavirus cases have been recorded, and 1,243 deaths. A total of 35,075 people are currently in hospital with Covid-19, an increase of 22 percent compared to a week ago.

To date, the virus has killed almost two million people around the world, and more than 90 million infections have been recorded. Such sobering numbers.

13TH JANUARY

Three frontline health workers in their thirties have described the debilitating and life-changing effects of long Covid, the symptoms of which include painful palpitations, chronic diarrhoea, brain fog and only being able to walk short distances.

The UK has recorded its highest increase in Covid deaths, with 1,564 being announced in the past 24 hours. The total death toll is now above 84,000. In a glimmer of hope, today is the third day running when new infections have been below 50,000.

From next week, people arriving in England must prove they have tested negative for the virus.

14TH JANUARY

WHO scientists have arrived in Wuhan to investigate the origins of the pandemic and the claims that the virus jumped from animals to humans. The team will spend around a month in the Chinese city, where Covid-19 first emerged over a year ago.

The UK's largest temporary morgue will open in London to cope with rising coronavirus deaths. Meanwhile, another one that was set up in a former aircraft hangar in Norwich during the first wave of the pandemic has been put into use for the first time.

In the past 24 hours, the UK has recorded 48,682 new cases and 1,248 deaths. The UK how has the fifth-highest death rate in the world.

A UK study has concluded that people who have had Covid-19 are likely to be protected from reinfection for at least five months. The study also found that around six in 10 people who were reinfected were asymptomatic.

15TH JANUARY

One of two Brazilian coronavirus variants has been detected in the UK.

Global coronavirus deaths have passed two million, just over a year since the outbreak began. Deaths hit one million on 29th September, meaning the death toll has taken just 108 days to effectively double.

Ice cream contaminated with Covid-19 has been discovered in China. Initial epidemiological investigations indicate the company produced the batch of ice cream using raw materials including milk powder imported from New Zealand and whey powder imported from Ukraine. The cold temperature that the ice cream was stored at, coupled with the fact it contains fat, could explain why the virus had survived on the samples taken. A virologist said, "We shouldn't panic that every ice cream is suddenly contaminated with coronavirus... The chances are this is a result of an issue with the production plant and potentially down to hygiene at the factory."

The company's 1,662 employees have been placed under quarantine.

Here in the UK, the R number is estimated to be between 1.2 and 1.3. A further 55,761 cases have been recorded, and 1,280 deaths.

17TH JANUARY

All adults in the UK will be offered their first dose of the Covid vaccine by September, and 10 new vaccination centres are due to open tomorrow. Today, I found out that a good friend of mine who lives near London has the virus. Her symptoms seem mild, just a cough and aches, but it's still worrying, and it's frustrating that there is nothing I can do to help her.

The UK has recorded a further 38,598 coronavirus cases and 671 deaths.

18TH JANUARY

A nurse has become the first person in Brazil to receive a coronavirus jab, just hours after the country's health regulator approved two vaccines for use.

The UK has recorded 37,535 new coronavirus cases and 599 deaths.

A total of 452,301 people have received their second vaccine dose.

19TH JANUARY

My thought for the day: While coronavirus is happening, we are helpless to help others and can only help ourselves, but by helping ourselves and not seeing other people, we *are* helping everyone else.

According to fresh antibody data from the ONS, an estimated one in eight people in England had had Covid-19 by December last year.

Our Health Secretary is self-isolating after receiving an alert from the NHS Covid-19 app to tell him he'd been in close contact with someone who has tested positive.

I feel for NHS staff. They have been dealing with this pandemic for nearly 10 months now, and they are almost on their knees.

The UK has recorded 33,355 new cases and 1,610 deaths, which is the highest daily figure in a single day since the pandemic began.

20TH JANUARY

Since the pandemic began, 93,290 people have now died in the UK, and 3,505,754 infections have been confirmed.

Meanwhile, a new study has found that the vaccines

being rolled out in the UK and around the world may be less effective against the new South African variant – known as 501Y.V2 – which contains mutations that may be resistant to immunity from previous coronavirus infection.

A separate study in China has been looking at how the virus spreads indoors. It found that talking face to face with one other person for just 15 minutes was enough time for the virus to be transmitted.

If someone's infected – maybe without realising it because they have no symptoms – they will release the virus as they breathe, especially if they cough. Most of it will be carried in droplets and fall to the ground, but if you're within two metres of them, it could reach your eyes, nose or mouth. The infected person will also release smaller particles called aerosols. Indoors, these can accumulate in the air and pose a hazard, though outside they should rapidly disperse. Walking past someone in the street or having a jogger run by you means you are close together for a few seconds at most. Fleeting encounters are highly unlikely to be long enough for the infection to reach you, though researchers in the USA found the virus on the handles of rubbish bins and on the buttons of pedestrian crossings.

The UK has recorded a further 38,905 coronavirus cases and 1,820 deaths.

22ND JANUARY

The UK has recorded 40,261 new cases and 1,401 deaths.

23RD JANUARY

I know six people who have recently tested positive for Covid. All of them seem OK; some have lost their sense of taste and smell, some are achy, but none of them needs hospital treatment, thank goodness.

Northern Ireland has extended its lockdown restrictions until 5th March.

Almost 5.4 million people in the UK have received their first dose of the Covid vaccination.

The UK's R number has dropped sharply to between 0.8 and 1, which suggests the current lockdown is working.

A further 33,552 coronavirus cases have been recorded and 1,348 deaths.

24TH JANUARY

Today was a Snow Day! By 10 am, there was a thick layer of snow outside, so we got our sled out and had loads of fun on it. We also made snow angels and had snowball fights. My daughter made a giant snowball and managed to throw it hard enough so that it catapulted the toy cat on her sled into the air. So funny.

The UK has hit another milestone in the Covid-19 pandemic, as the number of patients on a ventilator has passed 4,000 for the first time.

A further 30,004 cases have been recorded and 610 deaths.

25TH JANUARY

The UK has recorded its lowest daily rise in coronavirus cases since 15th December – 22,195. There have been an additional 592 deaths.

Scientists have said that vaccinating pets against Covid-19 could become necessary to stop the spread of the virus. A professor of evolutionary genetics said dogs and cats can contract coronavirus, although there are no known cases of them passing it on to humans.

In the city of Manaus, in Brazil, which is deep in the Amazon rainforest and where the Brazilian variant of Covid-19 is believed to have originated, conditions are now so bad that people are suffocating in hospital beds without oxygen. It is being described as like a "medieval plague", and there are fears that it is only going to continue to spread.

26TH JANUARY

In the UK, deaths linked to coronavirus have now surpassed 100,000.

Two people I know have told me that in the early stages of having Covid, they had sickness and an upset stomach. This could be a new symptom of the virus, as I haven't heard it mentioned anywhere before, but then the symptoms seem to be changing constantly.

Eight gorillas at San Diego Zoo Safari Park have caught the virus from one of the zookeepers.

The PM addressed the nation tonight and said he is deeply sorry for every life lost. He added that he took full responsibility for everything the government has done. He offered his deepest condolences to everyone who has lost a loved one: fathers, mothers, brothers, sisters, sons, daughters, and the many grandparents who have been taken.

On 11th November last year, the UK recorded 50,000 coronavirus-related deaths. It has taken just 76 days for that figure to double.

The Chief Medical Officer, Chris Whitty, warned there are quite a lot more deaths to come before the effects of the vaccines begin to be felt.

I also saw on the news that lots of people are being fined for breaking lockdown rules. Some people's excuse was that they weren't aware of a global pandemic. Really? How could they have missed that? It's all anyone has talked about for an entire year!

A study has found that people infected with the new coronavirus variant discovered in the UK are less likely to report losing their sense of taste and smell. However, other symptoms, such as a cough, sore throat, fatigue, muscle ache and fever were more common among those who had caught the new variant.

A further 25,308 new coronavirus cases have been recorded in the UK and 1,725 deaths. In total, 7.1 million people have now received their first dose of the Covid vaccine.

Hopefully, schools can reopen again from 8th March.

28TH JANUARY

A further 29,079 new coronavirus cases have been recorded and 245 deaths.

29TH JANUARY

The lockdown in Wales has been extended for at least three more weeks. The UK's R number is now between 0.7 and 1.1

30TH JANUARY

I felt really down yesterday. During the first two lockdowns, I was upbeat and generally positive, but this time round I'm not really enjoying it. I'm rubbish at home schooling, and it's exhausting and frustrating. I miss going out to dinner and to the cinema, and I miss my friends. I also worry about Angel. I spoke to her last night, and she is flying to Colombia and plans to stay there for a while. Colombia has more coronavirus cases, so I'll keep checking in with her to make sure she is OK. She has been fine so far, so I'm sure she will continue to be. I can't wait to hug her again.

The UK has recorded 23,275 new cases and 1,200 deaths.

31ST JANUARY

My life comprises an assortment of binge eating, comfort eating, boredom eating… whatever you want to call it. I'm looking forward to burning it off at kickboxing when the lockdown is over.

Captain Sir Tom Moore, the Second World War veteran who was knighted after raising millions of pounds for the NHS during the UK's first lockdown, has been admitted to hospital with breathing problems after testing positive for coronavirus.

The UK has recorded a further 21,088 cases and 587 deaths.

1ST FEBRUARY

Almost 9.3 million people have now received the first dose of the Covid vaccine.

Today, it was revealed that 105 cases of the South African Covid variant have been identified in the UK. In an attempt to halt the spread of the strain, the government has announced that coronavirus testers will go door to door across a number of areas of England to swab 80,000 people.

The UK has recorded 18,607 new cases and 406 deaths.

The total death toll stands at 106,564, and almost four million people have tested positive for the virus so far.

2ND FEBRUARY

Today is Angel's birthday. I FaceTimed her and she was in high spirits, which is hardly surprising considering she is in a beautiful country, enjoying beautiful weather and witnessing beautiful things. It was lovely to see her and have a chat. I wish we had been celebrating in person.

The number of Covid deaths in the second wave has now exceeded the first.

Captain Sir Tom Moore has sadly passed away.

3RD FEBRUARY

Ten million people have now had the first dose of a Covid vaccine in the UK, and 498,962 people have had two doses.

A German veterinary clinic has trained sniffer dogs to detect coronavirus in human saliva samples – with 94 percent accuracy. The dogs have been trained to pick up the 'corona odour' that comes from the cells of infected people.

Scientists have discovered that variants of Covid-19 that have the E48K mutation could reduce the efficiency of vaccines, although the jabs are still expected to provide good protection against illness and severe disease. Experts are now working to tweak the vaccines to increase their effectiveness against mutations. The E48K mutation is present in the variants first identified in South Africa and Kent.

The coronavirus infection rate in the UK is still alarmingly high, though the PM has said we are past the current peak. He also hailed the UK's milestone of having administered 10 million first doses of the Covid-19 vaccine.

Tonight, the country showed its thanks to the hero Captain Sir Tom Moore by clapping on their doorsteps. Doctors, nurses and the PM all joined in. Firefighters switched on the blue lights on their trucks and boats tooted their horns. I stood on my doorstep and clapped while my daughter banged a drum. What an inspirational person the nation has lost.

There have been 19,202 new coronavirus cases and 1,322 deaths.

7TH FEBRUARY

A total of 12 million people have now received their first dose of the Covid vaccine.

The UK has recorded 15,845 new coronavirus cases and 373 deaths.

There was more snow today – not loads, but enough to put a smile on my daughter's face. That's good enough for me.

8TH FEBRUARY

The UK has recorded 14,104 new cases and 333 deaths.

9TH FEBRUARY

Figures released by the ONS show there were 19 consecutive days in January when the daily death toll was above 1,000.

The WHO has discounted the theory that the Covid-19 virus came from a lab, saying it is "extremely unlikely".

The UK has recorded 12,364 new cases and 1,052 deaths.

11TH FEBRUARY

Under new border measures, everyone entering the country will be required to take a test on day two and day eight following their arrival, as part of a 10-day quarantine period.

I read today how double masking could be the way forward in containing the virus. A report from the Centers for Disease Control and Prevention (CDC) in the US suggested that putting a cloth mask over a medical mask could reduce the wearer's exposure to virus-sized particles by upwards of 90 percent. If two people both double mask, the risk of the virus getting from one to the other is reduced by 96.4 percent.

The UK has recorded a further 13,494 new cases and 678 deaths.

13TH FEBRUARY

The Oxford-AstraZeneca vaccine is to be tested on children as young as six in a world-first trial. Researchers will use 300 volunteers to assess whether the vaccine will produce a strong immune response in children aged between six and 17.

Almost 14.6 million people have now received their first vaccine.

The UK has recorded 13,308 new cases and 621 deaths.

15TH FEBRUARY

The UK has recorded 9,765 new cases and 230 deaths.

16TH FEBRUARY

Today, my daughter and I reverted to a habit we picked up in the first lockdown and made some rocky road. As it was raining, there was not much to do. The novelty of the lockdown is rapidly wearing off.

The UK has recorded 10,625 new cases and 799 deaths.

17TH FEBRUARY

It's been reported that every UK adult should have received both Covid jabs by August. Almost 16 million people have had their first dose.

The UK has recorded 12,718 new cases and 738 deaths.

19TH FEBRUARY

Today, my daughter and I went on a four-mile walk; it wasn't too cold, and we'd both been going a bit stir crazy in the house and needed a distraction and some fresh air. Two hours or so later, we reached a bakery and rewarded ourselves for walking so far with a pink iced bun. We were both covered in mud, but the walk was so much fun, and we were laughing so much that it didn't really bother us.

The UK has recorded 12,027 new coronavirus cases and 533 deaths.

21ST FEBRUARY

Another walk today. Not such a long one this time, as my daughter insisted on wearing shorts, a vest and a sweatband because she wanted to be a jogger. It was too cold, but she did it anyway. She ran alongside cyclists while shouting, "I'm winning, I'm winning!" She is so funny. When we came home, Dave made pancakes and we topped them with squirty cream, strawberries, blueberries and grapes.

22ND FEBRUARY

The UK has recorded 10,641 new coronavirus cases and 178 deaths.

23RD FEBRUARY

Boris Johnson has set out the dates for a four-step roadmap to easing the lockdown. Each step will be determined by Covid data. I feel relieved these steps to normality are being taken, but also a bit apprehensive, as I don't know if we are ready for it yet.

A maximum of six people or two households will be able to meet outside, including in private gardens, from 29th March.

The next step will be to reopen beer gardens and hairdressers in England, from 12th April at the earliest.

Non-essential shops, nail salons and gyms are also set to reopen, along with libraries, museums, zoos and theme parks.

From 17th May at the earliest, pubs, restaurants, cinemas and hotels will be allowed to open. Most rules on social contact outdoors will be lifted, while the mixing of different households will be allowed indoors. Up to 30 people will be permitted at weddings, funerals, wakes, receptions and christenings.

From 21st June at the earliest, all legal limits on social contact are set to be removed, with the remaining sectors of the economy, including nightclubs, reopened. Ministers also plan to decide on whether the existing restrictions on weddings can be lifted. The government has also said testing could be used to ensure people can safely attend large events.

The plan to reopen schools in England is going ahead on 8th March. On the same date, outdoor recreation with one other person will also be permitted, meaning people will be allowed to sit together in a park and enjoy a coffee, drink or picnic.

Meanwhile, the USA has become the first country to record more than half a million Covid-related deaths. More than 28 million people in the country have tested positive.

A study carried out in Wuhan has shown that nearly a quarter of Covid-19 patients suffer from hair loss within six months of becoming infected, with women at greater risk.

The UK has recorded 8,489 new cases and 548 deaths.

24TH FEBRUARY

The UK has recorded 9,938 new cases and 442 deaths.

25TH FEBRUARY

More than 18.6 million people have now had their first dose of the Covid vaccine in the UK. A total of 700,000 have had their second jab.

The UK has recorded 9,985 new cases and 323 deaths.

28TH FEBRUARY

New Zealand's Prime Minister, Jacinda Ardern, has announced that the country's biggest city, Auckland, will go into a seven-day lockdown following the detection of a single Covid-19 case. New Zealand is one of the most successful developed nations in controlling the spread of the virus, having confirmed barely over 2,000 cases since the pandemic began.

Another variant of concern has been discovered in the UK. Three cases of the new variant, known as P1, which originated in Brazil, are understood to have been detected in England, and the Scottish government has said it has found three cases in the north of the country.

Secondary school and college students will be tested for Covid twice a week when they return to the classroom on 8th March. Primary school children will not be tested, as scientists say there is no evidence of high transmission among this younger age group.

We went to the woods today and climbed trees and did some bug hunting.

The UK has recorded 6,035 new cases and 144 deaths.

1ST MARCH

The UK has recorded 5,455 new cases and 104 deaths.

3RD MARCH

Brazil has recorded 1,641 deaths in just one day. The South American country has the second highest coronavirus death toll after the United States.

4TH MARCH

Today was my birthday. People sent cards, flowers and left presents on my doorstep, which I thought was lovely.

You know old age is setting in when you look at yourself in the mirror and need to put on your glasses because your face is a bit blurry! The bags under your eyes are dark and mysterious, and around them are crinkles that have seemingly come out of nowhere and make you look tired and unyouthful. Does ageing creep up gradually until one day, when you are not darting here and there and juggling 20 million things, you stop to have a proper look at yourself, and you realise that this is what being middle-aged is all about?

Nearly 21 million people in the UK have now had their first vaccine jab.

6TH MARCH

The UK has recorded 6,040 new cases and 158 deaths.

7TH MARCH

My daughter goes back to school tomorrow. I am a little bit nervous, but I'm hoping everything will be OK. She definitely needs this; firstly for her education and secondly for her mental health.

The UK has recorded 5,177 new cases, which is a drop of around 850 from last Sunday.

8TH MARCH

The house felt so quiet today without my daughter here, and I was counting down the hours until I could pick her up. She came home full of beans, which was a relief.

For the second day running, the UK has recorded fewer than 100 coronavirus deaths.

9TH MARCH

NHS Nightingale Hospitals are set to close. They are no longer required after existing hospitals increased their bed capacity.

It has been revealed that the Pfizer/BioNTech coronavirus vaccine *is* able to combat the P.1 variant of Covid-19, which originated in Brazil. Scientists tested the blood of people who had received the jab and found it fared well against a laboratory-made version of the variant.

10TH MARCH

The UK has recorded 5,926 cases and 190 deaths.

12TH MARCH

Thailand has said it will delay the use of the Oxford-AstraZeneca vaccine following the decision by several European countries to temporarily suspend giving it out, after a small number of reports of blood clots. The European Medicines Agency (EMA) has backed the jab's safety and said there have been only 30 reports of blood clots among close to five million people receiving the vaccine across Europe.

Coronavirus restrictions on people meeting outdoors have been eased in Scotland. Four people from two households can now meet outdoors.

Italy is set to impose another national lockdown over the Easter weekend to combat growing numbers of coronavirus cases.

Wales will allow hair salons to open from Monday, but non-essential shops will remain closed.

A milestone has been reached in America, as more than 100 million vaccine doses have been administered across the country. Around 35 million people are fully vaccinated, accounting for 13.5 percent of the adult population.

Here in the UK, the number of people who have had

their first vaccine dose is 23.3 million, while almost 1.5 million have had their second one.

Greece is set to further extend restrictions in Athens and other areas to rein in the spread of the virus and ease pressure on its stretched health system.

The UK has recorded 6,609 cases and 175 deaths.

The Covid infection rate in England has hit the lowest level since September, and the R number has fallen to between 0.6 and 0.8.

14TH MARCH

Ireland has temporarily halted its use of the Oxford-AstraZeneca vaccine. The move came after a review from the Norwegian Medicines Agency showed four new cases of blood clotting in adults had occurred after receiving the jab.

16TH MARCH

Following further concerns over the side effects of Covid-19 vaccines, and the decision of more countries, including Lithuania and Latvia, to suspend their vaccine roll-outs, AstraZeneca says it has completed a review examining how safe its vaccine is. This was based on data covering the 17 million people who have been vaccinated in the UK and the EU. They concluded there was "no evidence of an increased risk of pulmonary embolism, deep vein thrombosis, or thrombocytopenia in any defined age group, gender, batch or in any particular country."

A professor at the London School of Hygiene and Tropical Medicine has pointed out that it is difficult to distinguish between causal effect and coincidence, especially considering that Covid-19 is strongly associated with blood clotting.

I spoke to Angel today. She is due to come home from Colombia at the end of April. I'm counting the days. It feels like she has been gone forever.

Scotland's stay-at-home order is to end on 2nd April, with a phased reopening of non-essential retail beginning three days later.

My daughter continues to crack me up. Tonight, she said, "Have we got any prawn cocktail sticks?" and later, "Oh, look, it's pebble-stoning."

The UK has confirmed 5,294 new coronavirus cases and 110 deaths.

17TH MARCH

More than 25 million people in the UK have now had their first dose of the Covid vaccine.

18TH MARCH

A rigorous scientific review has found no evidence that the Oxford-AstraZeneca vaccine causes blood clots. As a consequence, Italy, Latvia and Lithuania have decided to resume their vaccine roll-outs. Sweden says it will take a decision about its paused programme next week.

Paris is among 16 French regions set to go into a month-long lockdown from midnight tomorrow. Under the latest measures, schools will remain open, but all non-essential shops will be required to close.

19TH MARCH

Boris Johnson received his first dose of the Oxford-AstraZeneca vaccine.

21ST MARCH

The UK has broken its vaccine record for a third day in a row, with 873,784 jabs administered yesterday and 756,873 administered today.

22ND MARCH

The UK has recorded 5,342 new coronavirus cases and 17 deaths.

23RD MARCH

A year to the day since the UK was plunged into its first lockdown, more than 28 million people in the UK have had their first vaccine.

On a more sombre note, people observed a minute's silence to remember the victims of the pandemic. At 8 pm people stood on their doorsteps with phones, candles and torches to signify a 'beacon of remembrance'.

The London Eye, Tate Britain, Blackpool Tower, Belfast City Hall and Liverpool Town Hall were among the landmarks lit up in yellow to mark the occasion, and the Queen made a heartfelt speech. I felt sad that we had got this far with so many losses. At least they were acknowledged, but I just want this whole thing to be over, and for there to be no more deaths. It's the uncertainty that's the most worrying.

Latest figures from the ONS reveal that since the pandemic began, a total of 149,117 people have had coronavirus recorded on their death certificate.

The UK recorded 5,379 new cases and 112 deaths.

24TH MARCH

Brazil's daily Covid deaths have surpassed 3,000 for the first time.

There are reports of a 'double mutant' variant in India, which comes as the country records 47,262 new cases and 275 deaths.

Meanwhile, the UK has recorded 5,605 new cases and 98 deaths.

25TH MARCH

There are currently 4,000 patients being treated for coronavirus in UK hospitals, down from 34,000 in mid-January.

In other news, attempting to take a holiday abroad without a reasonable excuse will result in a hefty fine. If the new UK law is approved, it will come into effect on 29th March and run until 30th June. The Health Secretary has suggested foreign holidays could still be allowed before that date.

The UK has recorded 6,397 new cases and 63 deaths.

26TH MARCH

Scientists are planning to test the effectiveness of the Oxford-AstraZeneca vaccine when it's administered using a nasal spray. As part of the study, the researchers will examine the level of immune response when administering the shot through the nose, as well as monitoring the safety of this method and any adverse reactions.

I came down with a cold today. Nowadays, the common cold might be something else, so I did a rapid lateral flow test, which takes 30 mins for a result. Thankfully, it came back negative.

Almost 30 million people in the UK have now had their first vaccine.

27TH MARCH

The UK has recorded 4,715 new coronavirus cases and 58 deaths.

31ST MARCH

The Irish government has announced some easing of its strict lockdown restrictions. These will begin from mid-April and include allowing two fully vaccinated people to meet indoors.

The UK has recorded 4,040 new cases and 56 deaths.

The Pfizer vaccine has been deemed safe and 100 percent effective in children aged 12 to 15.

1ST APRIL

Latest figures show a total of 1.1 million people in the UK have reported suffering from long Covid.

France has entered its third national lockdown.

UK coronavirus numbers are continuing to fall. A total of 4,479 new cases have been recorded and 51 deaths.

2ND APRIL

Turkey has reported its highest number of daily coronavirus cases so far, with a total of 42,308 new infections being recorded.

Closer to home, the R number is estimated to be

between 0.8 and 1.0.

Eighteen million people in the UK have received a Covid jab, and there are 30 reports of people suffering blood clots.

A total of 3,402 new coronavirus cases have been recorded and 52 deaths.

4TH APRIL

The UK has recorded 3,423 new cases and 10 deaths. Finally, a low death count. Let's hope it drops completely and we can beat this awful virus for good.

5TH APRIL

New cases of Covid-19 in India have surged passed 100,000 a day – the highest total of daily cases recorded in the country since the pandemic began. More than 103,790 new infections were announced recently, taking the total number of coronavirus cases in India to over 12.5 million.

7TH APRIL

More than 4,000 Covid deaths have been recorded in a single day in Brazil. The more contagious Manaus variant of the disease, coupled with a lack of lockdown restrictions, have left Brazil's outbreak to spiral out of control. A total of 86,979 new cases were recorded in the country yesterday, along with 4,195 deaths.

The Moderna vaccine has been administered for the first time in the UK.

India has recorded 115,000 new cases.

More than 5.6 million people in the UK have now had both doses of a coronavirus vaccine.

11TH APRIL

England's coronavirus restrictions will be eased further tomorrow, with pubs and restaurants allowed to serve people outdoors. Hairdressers will reopen, as will non-essential shops, indoor gyms, swimming pools, libraries, zoos and nail salons.

International holidays remain off the cards.

Households cannot mix indoors.

To help customers avoid crowds, shops will be able to extend their opening hours from 7 am to 10 pm.

The UK has recorded 1,730 new cases and 7 deaths.

12TH APRIL

Concerning the four steps to easing England's lockdown, Boris Johnson has said that he hopes to be able to lift the majority of the rules by 21st June, but this is dependent on cases, deaths and hospital admissions continuing to fall. So, the dates that have been provided are the earliest any of the stated rules can be lifted.

Firstly, there will be no regional tier system – in the easing of lockdown, England will be treated as one.

Step one was completed in two parts on 8th and 29th March after the PM confirmed the roadmap was on track thanks to the successful vaccine programme.

We are now progressing to the next planned stages of lockdown lifting, and the steps are as follows:

Step two, 12th April (today)

The opening of non-essential shops, indoor gyms, etc.

People are still barred from exercise classes. Museums, cinemas and children's play areas will remain closed.

Step three, 17th May

Outdoors, most social contact rules will be lifted, but

gatherings of more than 30 people will be illegal.

Indoors, the rule of six will be extended to allow larger groups of up to two households.

The lifting of restrictions on indoor hospitality will include serving inside in pubs and restaurants. Cinemas, theatres, museums, galleries, concert halls, children's play areas can reopen, and indoor exercise classes will be allowed.

Advice on social distancing between family and friends, including hugging, will be updated no later than 17th May.

Step four, 21st June

All legal limits on social contact to be removed. The government hopes to reopen nightclubs and lift restrictions on large events such as festivals. Testing could be used as a condition of entry.

Ministers hope to remove restrictions on weddings.

More than 7.6 million people in the UK have now received both doses of a coronavirus vaccine.

13TH APRIL

The Moderna vaccine is the most expensive per dose of the vaccines created so far.

The UK has recorded 2,472 new cases and 23 deaths.

14TH APRIL

India has witnessed a record number of cases, with 184,372 new infections recorded in the past 24 hours.

15TH APRIL

A further 200,000 new coronavirus cases have been recorded in India, as hospitals report severe shortages of beds and oxygen. Extra space is being provided in hotels.

18ᵀᴴ APRIL

More than 9.9 million people in the UK have now received both doses of a Covid-19 vaccine, while nearly 33 million have had their first dose.

In the UK, 1,882 new coronavirus cases were recorded along with 10 deaths.

19ᵀᴴ APRIL

New Delhi is entering a week-long lockdown to prevent the collapse of the capital's health system amid India's nationwide coronavirus surge. Delhi recently recorded over 25,000 new cases and 161 deaths, making it the worst affected city in the country.

India's double mutation virus is thought to be fuelling this deadly second wave. The India variant, officially called B.1.617, is a combination of two mutations – E484Q and L452R – and was first detected last year. Apparently, it has the hallmarks of being extremely dangerous, as the two new significant mutations in the spike protein help it to infect cells and evade the immune system.

So far, India has registered the highest number of coronavirus cases in the world. More than 15 million people have contracted the virus, making it the second worst affected country after the USA. At least 182 cases of the India variant have been detected in the UK, 162 of which were identified in the last five weeks.

In other UK news, more than 10 million people – one in five adults – have now received both doses of a Covid-19 vaccine. At total of 2,963 new cases have been recorded, and four deaths.

20TH APRIL

I spoke to Angel tonight and she is coming home on 30th April (dances while writing). She must self-isolate at home for 10 days after arriving, but I can't wait to see her when she is free. I'm glad she is safe. Thank goodness Covid didn't get its claws into her. Thinking about it, maybe I should have gone with her; I could have done with six months in a beautiful country. Hopefully, Covid will go away soon because I'd really appreciate a bit of normality right now.

The UK has recorded 2,524 new cases and 33 deaths.

22ND APRIL

India has recorded more than 300,000 new coronavirus cases in a 24-hour period, and a further 2,104 deaths.

Angel messaged me tonight to tell me that after experiencing cold symptoms for the past couple of days, she took a precautionary Covid test, which came back positive. When I read her message, I got a pang in my heart, and I kept hearing the word positive over and over in my head. I felt sick to my stomach as panic set in. Questions raced around in my head. Is she OK? What if her condition worsens? How can I get to her when there's a travel ban in place? I phoned her, but she didn't pick up, and I felt my stomach flip. This wasn't a good sign. Luckily, she phoned me back five minutes later. She said she feels OK, and her symptoms are just like a regular cold with an accompanying headache. She says she doesn't know where she caught the virus, but she won't be able to come back now on her planned date. I told her I hope she will continue to be OK and that I love her very much. I then explained about long Covid and how she might start to feel really tired, and to look after herself. I didn't want the phone call to end, and

240

when it did, I felt so helpless. I need her to be OK. With so many new variants flying around, who knows which one she has – let's hope it's one that causes mild symptoms throughout. I couldn't help shedding a tear. I cried because it was out of my control and because I don't want to lose my friend. My brain was going into overdrive, and I thought how if anything happens to her out there, my last memory of her will be hugging her and saying goodbye before she left for Costa Rica. My heart hurt when I thought of this.

23RD APRIL

A total of 55 new cases of the Indian double mutant variant have been found in the UK.

Hospitals across India are filling up with people battling the virus, and they are reaching breaking point amid a shortage of oxygen, beds and medicines. Tragically, people are dying on the pavements while waiting for a hospital bed to free up. It's so hard watching this on the TV; my heart goes out to these people. It also terrifies me that we could get to this point, too. The awful thing about this virus, and every country battling it, is that we can't help each other because we are struggling to help ourselves.

Today alone, India recorded 330,000 new cases and 2,263 deaths.

Meanwhile, Japan has declared a third state of emergency to try and combat its surge in coronavirus cases.

Experts have said that people can catch Covid twice, even after being vaccinated, and they can still transmit the virus to others.

In other coronavirus news, researchers have identified two cases of human-to-cat transmission. The cats, of different breeds, were living in separate households and displayed mild to severe respiratory symptoms. The first cat was a four-month-old female ragdoll kitten that fell ill in March 2020, and the second was a six-year-old female Siamese. Researchers believe both pets were infected by their owners, who had suffered with Covid-19 symptoms before the cats became unwell. The study also reiterated there is currently no evidence of cat-to-human transmission or that domestic animals can spread the infection.

The UK has recorded 2,678 new cases and 40 deaths.

24TH APRIL

In Delhi, more than 26,000 new Covid cases and 306 deaths have been recorded in the past 24 hours.

26TH APRIL

Portugal has recorded no daily deaths for the first time since August 2020.

27TH APRIL

The UK has recorded 2,685 new coronavirus cases and 17 deaths. The total death toll now stands at 127,451.

1ST MAY

Angel was about to sit on the toilet in Costa Rica when she saw a claw and some movement. A huge crab had got itself stuck in the pan. I said to her it would have been very amusing if she hadn't noticed and it had nipped her bottom. Anyway, to cut a long story short, the crab was rescued and set free. Hopefully, it will go on to live a long and happy life.

3RD MAY

A total of 1,649 new coronavirus cases have been recorded, along with one death. More than 50 million doses of the vaccine have now been administered.

4TH MAY

The number of coronavirus infections in India has passed 20 million, with 357,229 new cases reported in the last 24 hours.

NHS England has said it will be ready to give Britons a third jab from September.

7TH MAY

A coronavirus strain first detected in India has been declared a "variant of concern" by Public Health England, after cases more than doubled in a week. The strain is one of three related variants first identified in India. Almost half the cases are related to travel or contact with a traveller.

9TH MAY

Yay, Angel landed back in the UK today! It's such a relief to know she is OK. She has to self-isolate for 10 days, so we can't see each other just yet, but I have waited this long, so I can wait a little longer. She is safe, and she is home, and for now, that is enough to keep me happy. She has tested negative for Covid but will need to take two more tests while she's in isolation.

18TH MAY

I had my first Covid jab today – the Pfizer one. I waited in line and then sat down with a nurse, answered some questions, had the jab and then sat in a waiting room for 15 minutes just in case I had a reaction. Stage one complete.

Fifty doctors have died in India in a single day. Coronavirus cases there have now surpassed 25 million.

19TH MAY

Almost 3,000 cases of the Indian variant have been recorded in the UK. The government's scientific advisers have warned there is a realistic possibility it could be 50 percent more transmissible than the variant that emerged in Kent late last year and led to England's third lockdown.

1ST JUNE

The UK has recorded zero deaths. I was so happy when I heard this, and I hope it's a sign we are finally coming out the other side. I feel the news is worth celebrating, as it's taken three lockdowns to get to this point. The cases are still high because of the Indian variant, but one step at a time.

6TH JUNE

We took my daughter to a trampoline park today, as she plans to hold her birthday party at one and wanted to take a look. She loved it, and as an added bonus, it was practically empty.

Cases seem to be rising fast. I hope they don't spiral out of control again, as restrictions are meant to be easing later this month.

In better news, Angel came over to see us. As soon as I saw her, I gave her the biggest hug. I have no idea how long I held her for, but I know I didn't want to let go. I have waited so long for that cuddle.

11TH JUNE

Just over 80 people currently in hospital with the Indian variant are fully vaccinated.

In total, the UK has recorded 8,125 new coronavirus cases and 17 deaths.

19TH JUNE

For the third consecutive day, the UK has recorded more than 10,000 Covid cases.

I've started back at kickboxing, which is really refreshing as it means I can mentally focus on something other than the virus and get my fitness back. Dave has finally had his operation, which he has been waiting a year and a half for, and now he is back at home and will spend the next eight weeks recovering.

Angel came over and we went for a walk and then had lunch. Back when we were 18 and living at the hostel, our favourite film to watch together was *Kickboxer*. There's a part in the film when Jean-Claude van Damme dances, and Angel would always get up and dance along with him. Well, fast forward 20 years and after lunch I put the film on while Angel was in the kitchen. I paused it at the appropriate part and called her into the living room. Then, like clockwork, as soon as I pressed play, she started to dance. It's moments like this that truly make me appreciate our friendship. In another 20 years' time, I guarantee that I will put the film on, and history will repeat itself.

4TH JULY, 2022

I had to take a break from writing about coronavirus, as it consumed my thoughts and life and became somewhat of an unhealthy obsession. To date, my family hasn't had Covid, thankfully, but it seems everyone around us has come down with it at some point. Angel has had it twice now, and most people seem resigned to living with it. Thanks to the vaccines, people are not being hospitalised as much as they were at the start of all this, and daily death tolls are no longer part of the news, thank goodness.

I'm not as scared of Covid as I was when it started, which is a good thing, as I think it's inevitable I will get it eventually.

25TH SEPTEMBER, 2022

Covid has calmed down massively, and normality has returned… finally. You hardly hear of it now, and there are no more masks, hand sanitisers, social distancing and uncertainty. I still haven't had it – as far as I'm aware – so either I have been super-careful or lucky, or I'm immune. Either way, I'm just glad the pandemic is pretty much over. The whirlwind that swept everyone up is something that is going to be remembered for a long time. Every country's and every person's story will be different, but for a time, we were all in it together, whether we wanted to be or not. I hope it doesn't come back, and that we will never have to go through anything like it again.

Hopefully, my diary is something that can be looked back on and maybe shown to future generations, who will struggle to imagine the world as they know it shutting down.

Afterword

So, that's it, you are all up to date with my life. I shall close by saying this…

I've been through some truly traumatic experiences in my life, and if Dave hadn't saved me from myself, who knows where I would have ended up? I still feel there are other people who have been through worse. I don't think I'm better than anyone else, or that my life experiences are somehow harder than anybody else's; we all deal with things at our own pace and in our own way. I do believe that just because someone has done something bad to you doesn't mean you have to copy that behaviour and be bad to the people around you.

Do I miss my mother? No, I miss the thought of having a mother. I've missed out on that experience. Do I miss my father? Never!

Sometimes, if I get upset, I push my internal self-destruct button. I will eat badly, or drink a little too much, but none of us is perfect. I am lucky to have good friends and an amazing husband who sticks by me. I try to keep people by my side who love me regardless and who bring out the best in me. In my experience, these kinds of people are key. And cats. Cats are *always* good to have around.

I laugh a lot because – as the pandemic demonstrated – you never know when bad stuff is waiting around the corner. Life is hard, and that's just how it is. We are all going through something, but at different times.

I've been with Dave now for 20 years, and I couldn't be happier. Our beautiful, crazy daughter is nine and I love her more than words can say. I have three cats who mean the world to me, and this is my normal. This is the family I have always wanted. I also have my lifelong friends, whom I also count as family. What more could I want?

So, that's it. Now I'm doing life the same as everyone else. I don't feel so abnormal these days. People say I'm a little crazy, but I think it's a good crazy. I'm doing day-to-day things like the next person, while keeping my emotional baggage locked away in little boxes inside my head. Of course, I can never rid myself of the memories completely, but I'm making better ones to replace them, and I will continue to do so.

For me, that is enough.

I'm Amelia Hendrey, thank you for reading my story.

Twice.

ACKNOWLEDGMENTS

I'd like to take this opportunity to thank my editor and publisher, Danielle Wrate, who has been fantastic from start to finish. She saw the road I wanted to go down with the book and only wanted to help make it better. She was there throughout the entire process to answer my questions and listen to my ideas.

ABOUT THE AUTHOR

Amelia Hendrey is also the author of *What Nobody Knew*. She lives in Hertfordshire with her husband, daughter and four cats. When she is not writing, she works as a professional cat sitter.

If you enjoyed *Let Go of What You Know*, please leave a review on Amazon or Goodreads. You can also follow Amelia on Facebook.

 facebook.com/ameliahendreyauthor

Printed in Great Britain
by Amazon

17089105R00150